Science in a Social Context

Research and Technology as Economic Activities

Kenneth Green
Department of Liberal Studies in Science,
University of Manchester

Clive Morphet
Newcastle-upon-Tyne Polytechnic

Butterworths

LONDON - BOSTON
Sydney - Wellington - Durban - Toronto

The Butterworth Group

United Kingdom London	Butterworth & Co (Publishers) Ltd 88 Kingsway, WC2B 6AB
Australia Sydney	Butterworths Pty Ltd 586 Pacific Highway, Chatswood, NSW 2067 Also at Melbourne, Brisbane, Adelaide and Perth
South Africa Durban	Butterworth & Co (South Africa) (Pty) Ltd 152—154 Gale Street
New Zealand Wellington	Butterworths of New Zealand Ltd 26—28 Waring Taylor Street, 1
Canada Toronto	Butterworth & Co (Canada) Ltd 2265 Midland Avenue, Scarborough, Ontario, M1P 4S1
USA Boston	Butterworth (Publishers) Inc 19 Cummings Park, Woburn, Mass. 01801

First published 1977
ISBN 0 408 71300 3

Library of Congress Cataloging in Publication Data

Green, Kenneth.
    Research & technology as economic activities.

    Bibliography: p.
    1. Research, Industrial. I. Morphet, Clive,
joint author. II. Title.
HD30.4.G73   338.5'1   76-51316
ISBN 0-408-71300-3

Typeset by Scribe Design, Chatham, Kent
Printed in England by Chapel River Press, Andover, Hants.

:tion

Our technological future will be determined by choices made by institutions as to the rate and direction of technological activity. While political processes will always very clearly rule the choice of technologies of power and prestige (like defense or aerospace), the technologies of production and of consumer goods (and the associated researches which we will identify as 'economically-orientated') are developed within a framework of economic constraints: a framework within which return compared to capital invested is seen as the governing criterion for the decisions of the individual corporation, and within which economic growth is seen as the governing criterion for public policy. Our intention in this book is to locate the processes of research and technology within this economic framework, and thus to provide a concise introduction to an area of study which is of growing importance.

The focus is on the privately owned industrial organisation within an economy which is primarily capitalist — the UK provides most of our material. We review the following sorts of questions to which economists have addressed themselves:
1. Why do industrial firms do Research and Development (R & D) at all?
2. Why do some firms and industries spend more on R & D than others?
3. What factors affect the rate at which new products and processes spread through industry?
4. How do firms select an appropriate strategy or research policy which will balance their short and long term profitability against what it is technically possible for them to do?

Our intention has been to produce a fairly self-contained book which assumes no detailed knowledge on the reader's part of either economic or of statistical terms. There are at least two excellent orthodox texts which cover similar ground to that which we cover in this book: Norris, K. and Vaizey, J. (1973). *The Economics of Research and Technology*, (1968) George Allen and Unwin, and Mansfield, E. (1968). *The Economics of Technological Change*, New York, Norton. We make frequent reference to these books in our text. In addition we make frequent reference to, and strongly recommend Freeman, C. (1974). *The Economics of Industrial Innovation*, London, Penguin.

Freeman's book is concerned to point out, and to begin to explore, the wide range of options which technology makes available to the firm within the broad constraints of the economic system. In brief, his analysis points to a theory of the firm in which the environment to which it responds is one of world technology as well as world prices of inputs and outputs. This greatly widens the options open. In addition, the uncertainty which characterises the development of new knowledge makes the planning of research and innovation an activity which cannot be wholly governed by rational investment criteria. Whereas the firm described by the classical economist supposedly responds primarily to consumer choices, in the firm which exploits technology this mechanism breaks down — leading, Freeman claims, to the loss of 'consumer sovereignty'. The implication is drawn of the need for new mechanisms of public participation in the process of consumer-oriented innovation.

We hope that the directions typified by Freeman's work are the directions in which the study of this present text will lead. The issue is the determination of our future technologies. We discuss the economic constraints within which the firm operates, and we discuss some strategies for the firm's research policy. The processes by means of which research projects and technological innovations are selected within such strategies must be analysed in terms of the political structure of the industrial enterprise. Such an analysis is not presented here, but for indications as to where this study might lead see, as well as Freeman (1974), Elliott (1976).

After each chapter of this book a set of questions has been offered — these fall into two categories: 1. *Questions* — the answers to which are in the preceding text. They should be used by the reader for self assessment to see whether she/he has understood the key points which have been made. 2. *Points for discussion or essays* — which might be set as essay questions or used as the basis for discussions in seminars or tutorials. In Chapter 5 these appear throughout the text.

In Chapter 1 we introduce some basic definitions — of technology, innovation etc. — and show how they have been related to economic concepts, particularly that of the production function. From here we go on in Chapter 2 to look at the international and national contexts in which research in British industry is set. Chapter 3 examines some aspects of the economics of research and development on a national scale — in particular it looks at the relationship between research and development and economic growth. Chapters 4 and 5 move down from the national level to the level of the individual firm. Chapter 4 looks at R & D in British industry — which industries spend most on R & D and why? Chapter 5 is concerned to examine R & D in the firm. It is based on a pair of articles which describe the research policy of two large private companies — GEC and Philips — and we attempt to draw out of these articles some of the questions and some of the problems which relate to the way that these firms carry out their research and development activities.

Chapter One
Some Problems of Definition

If there were some common agreement on the meanings of the terms used in discussing the problems to which this unit is addressed then this section would look very different. We would list our terms — science, technology, technique, research, development etc. — and for each one we would give a definition. We would be careful to try and point out that these were consensual definitions and not absolute ones; nevertheless they would be true by virtue of the authority of common acceptance and you would reject them at your peril.

There is in fact little or no agreement about the precise meaning and usage of some of these terms. In this Chapter we will end up with the definitions that we propose to use in the course of this book but we do not wish to be dogmatic about them. We will mainly be concerned to explain what we mean when we use the word *technology*, and show how our meaning differs when we use the word *technique*.

There is a common usage of the word technology (and it is this common usage which enables us to use the word without confusion in the title of this unit) which relates to notions of fairly complex, perhaps 'scientific', machinery or ways of making or doing things. In line with this usage is the definition offered by Child (1969), who defines technology as:

> 'the equipment used in the workflow of a business enterprise and the interrelationship of the operations to which the equipment is applied'

We might note that this definition would include not only the machines themselves (the hardware) but also the organisational and management methods involved. This point is made even more clearly by Schon (1967), to whom technology is:

> 'any tool or technique, any product or process, any physical equipment or method of doing or making, by which human capability is extended'.

We do not find such definitions very satisfactory, mainly because they do not distinguish adequately between technology and technique.

The word technology owes its ending to the Greek word 'logos' which means something like science'. (cf. biology, psychology etc.) While we cannot set too much store by this point, particularly since what the Greeks meant by 'logos' cannot really correspond to what we mean by 'science', the notion of technology as *the science of technique'* (cf. biology 'the science of life processes') can be illuminating. We can operate for our present purposes with a dictionary definition of science as a branch of knowledge seeking to explain objects or experience through systematic study. If the object of study is technique, then *technology is the systematic knowledge of technique.*

Technique can be defined by relating it to the process by which all activities are carried out — the labor process. In this a man or a woman, individually or collectively, transform some object or set of objects ('raw materials') into another object ('the product'). He/she/they accomplish the transformation by the use of articles such as tools or machines. The interaction of the person, the tool and the object with the intent of producing some new object is the technique. *Technique:* the interaction of person(s)/tool or machine/object which defines a 'way of doing' a particular task.

Thus there can be several techniques by which a particular transformation of raw materials into products can be performed, and technology is the knowledge and understanding of this set of techniques.

Technology as the science of technique is therefore the scientific study of the relationships involved in the person/tool - machine/object complex.

It is our belief that the emphasis on technology as a *knowledge system* has particular implications for an understanding of the way in which technology relates to society and of the way in which it changes or 'advances'. The implications have really yet to be explored and are out of the scope of this book.

To sum up, the technology of a particular process or industry is the assemblage of all the craft, empirical and rational knowledge by which the techniques of that process or industry are understood and operated. An advance in technology, then, will involve the generation of new knowledge and the *addition of new techniques* to the set already available. We find this view of technology useful in the present context not least because it accords with the way in which some economists use the word — in particular Norris and Vaizey, whose book *The Economics of Research and Technology* has been mentioned in the Introduction. Their Chapter 1 ('Taxonomy') might be usefully compared with our own treatment.

In order to transpose our view into a more orthodox economic framework it is necessary to introduce some economic terms — and in particular to introduce the concept of the *production function.* Let us consider the manufacture of some item. This item is manu-factured by performing work on or using various 'materials' - some of these materials will be tools or machines, others will be inputs to the processes (objects of the labor process) which will emerge as the finished product. These materials the economist calls *capital*, the work that is performed on the objects with the tools or machines is *labor* and is contributed by workers employed for that purpose. *Capital* and *labor* are called, by economists, *factors of production*.

If we draw a pair of axes as in *Figure 1*, with capital inputs, (measured as the number of units of capital required to produce one unit of output) on the vertical axis and labor inputs (measured as the number of units of labor required to produce one unit of output) on the horizontal axis, we can put a point on this diagram which corresponds to that combination of capital and labor which needs to be deployed *using some specific technique* to manufacture each unit of output. This is point A_1 in *Figure 1*.

Figure 1   Production function for a *technique*   Figure 2   Production functions for a *set* of techniques

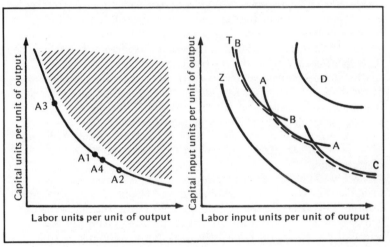

Labor units per unit of output   Labor input units per unit of output

Using this technique it will probably be possible to *substitute* to a certain extent either capital for labor or vice versa — eg. it might be possible to use one less machine if two men are put onto some other machine and work that machine harder. Thus, points A_2 and A_3 might also represent possible combinations of capital and labor, and in general all points on some line A will represent possible combinations of the factors of production. Since it is always possible to use inputs inefficiently, all combinations above and to the right of this line (shaded in *Figure 1*) will be technically possible. The line therefore represents the *boundary of technically efficient production possibilities*. A manufacturer will doubtless want to keep costs of production at a minimum and therefore will choose some point on

3

this boundary, say A_4, where total costs are at a minimum. The position of A_4 on the line will depend on the relative costs and labor.

Point A_4 then represents the *economically efficient production possibility*, given certain capital and labor costs.

The line through A_3, A_1, A_4 and A_2 is called the *production function* for technique A. In general output can be expressed as a function of labor and capital:

$$Q = f (L, K)$$

Where Q = output, L = labor input and K = capital input.

Now there will be other techniques which can be used to produce the item in question, and each will have an associated production function. This is shown in *Figure 2*. Again these are *boundaries of technically efficient production possibilities* and the manufacturer will choose to manufacture at some position on this set of boundaries which is economically the most efficient.

An efficient manufacturer will never use technique D but may use A, B, or C according to the relative costs of capital and labor.

The curve T (the envelope to curves A, B and C) is the boundary of technical efficiency, or *boundary production function*, following the appropriate sections of curves A, B and C, for the *overall set of techniques* available to the manufacturers.

We can now offer some definitions in economic terms which correspond to our usage of the word technology to mean the science of technique.

Technical change, or change in technique, will take place when a manufacturer stops using technique D and begins to use some other technique A, B or C because it is more efficient. Technical change will also be involved if a manufacturer, due to a change in the prices of capital and/or labor, moves from say technique A to technique B.

Technological change will take place when a new technique is introduced and added to the set of techniques available. It will involve an addition to the knowledge and understanding, the technology, of manufacture, for otherwise it would have been available before. Such a change might be represented by the production function Z in *Figure 2*. The boundary of technically efficient production has shifted down and to the left from T to Z.

Thus our definition of technology can be seen to correspond to the following definitions, used by economists:

Technical Change: A change in the technique chosen out of the available spectrum of techniques — often involving (as in movement along line T from lines A to B) a shift *along* the bounding production function. (But sometimes involving a movement from technical inefficiency on D to technical efficiency on T)

Technological Change: A change in the available set of techniques involving a shift of the bounding production function as in the movement of the boundary from T to Z.

It must be noted that any production function of the form $Q = f(L, K)$ is only true for one technique, or for one state of technology if it is a boundary production function.

Technological change is characterised by the *process of invention.* The development of, say, a new machine to perform a particular task will constitute invention — the new machine will constitute a new technique and thus will reflect a change in technology. We can also talk of *an invention* — this will be the machine itself, ie. the new technique. Thus we can define:

Invention as the process by which technology is changed, or the new technique generated by the process.

We can usually distinguish between the invention of a new technique and its actual embodiment in a production process. Thus power steering for motor vehicles was invented in the mid nineteen-twenties but not used until World War II when it was incorporated in many military vehicles. It was not until 1951 that power steering was made available by Chrysler and innovation might be considered to have occurred. Thus we can define:

Innovation as the first use (which is rarely immediate) of an invention or the embodiment of an invention in actual productive processes.

Research is a process of scientific enquiry which may be research in technology or research in one of the *pure sciences* such as physics. Because the boundaries between scientific disciplines are less than clear (also perhaps less than clearly understood) research in one area of science might have implications for some other area. Thus, research in physics will sometimes (although perhaps less often than might be imagined) have implications for technology; that is, it might have results which can be incorporated into techniques. Research carried out in anticipation of such applications is termed *applied research* or *applied science.* The term applied science is, we believe, also used to describe what we would prefer to call technological research; in fact it would be our contention that there is very little applied science which is not technological research. However our view of technology requires far more elaboration before this distinction can be substantiated.

In concluding this chapter of definitions we describe *development* as the activity involved in transforming a theoretical technological advance into concrete operational hardware. Development is usually the most costly and time consuming phase of the whole process by which innovation takes place.

Questions

1. On page 4 we say 'An efficient manufacturer will never use technique *D* but may use *A, B* or *C* according to the relative costs of capital and labor'. Why should this be so?
2. What's the difference between a technically efficient production possibility and an economically efficient production possibility?
3. Describe, in your own words, the distinction between a technical and a technological change.

Points for discussion or essays

1. The definitions given of technique and technology are not, as we have stated, supposed to be the final word on the subject. Below are some other definitions of these terms which have appeared in various books and articles. You might like to compare them with ours, see how they differ and discuss which is best.

   a) 'Technology is the systematic application of scientific or other organised knowledge of practical tasks'
   b) 'The term *technique*, as I use it, does not mean machines, technology, or this or that procedure for attaining an end. In our technological society *technique* is the *totality of methods rationally arrived at and having absolute efficiency* in *every* field of human activity.'
   c) 'Technology is the science of the industrial arts.'
   d) 'Technology is the term used to include all the scientific and engineering activities in the process of industrial innovation.'
   e) 'The term technology approximates very closely to the modern layman's name for what was previously and universally known as engineering.'
   f) 'Technology (is) a set of craft techniques.'
   g) 'Technology is an abstract concept embracing both tools and machines used by a society, and the relations between them implied by their use. It can be distinguished from 'technique', which will be taken as the act of applying knowledge, whether directly or with the aid of a tool or machine — that is with the aid of an element of technology — to a particular task.'

2. 'The relationships between technology, machine and technique might be seen as roughly equivalent to that between language, word and speech.' Do you agree?

3. In defining technological change as a shift of the bounding production function we have assumed that, as represented in our figures, the shift will be down and to the left. This assumes that technological change inevitably and inexorably introduces techniques which use less labor and less capital. However a new technique could, in principle, be introduced which uses much more labor and/or much more capital than any known technique. It would therefore be 'inefficient'.

But only because the concept of efficiency is defined in terms of the usage of capital and labor. The new 'inefficient' technique could in fact be 'better' than any other technique because it was, for example, more satisfying for those involved in doing it or was less environmentally disruptive. Thus it is important to remember that the production function concept, although useful in drawing distinctions between the various terms we are concerned with in this unit, has little to say about technological changes which are not describable in orthodox capitalist, market-economics terms.

Can you think of any examples of such 'inefficient' techniques? What does this problem tell us about the concepts of technical and economic efficiency? And about the production function?

Chapter Two
Research and Development in an International and National Context

Much of the material presented in this book is aimed at an understanding of the situation in the UK. It will also be specifically concerned with research and development (R & D) expenditure and activities which have an economic orientation — in other words, R & D intended to directly enhance the (industrial) production of material wealth. This section is designed to put this sector of R & D activity into a international and national context. We will try and attain an overall picture of the amounts of money spent on R & D in various countries, and of the several objectives which this expenditure is designed to meet. Also we will look at where the money comes from, and where it is spent.

Expenditure on R & D is concentrated in the most economically developed countries of the world, as will be evident from *Figure 3*; the figure also shows how R & D expenditure in the capitalist world

Figure 3   Share of total R & D expenditure accounted for by various countries — capitalist world. Estimated for 1966—7

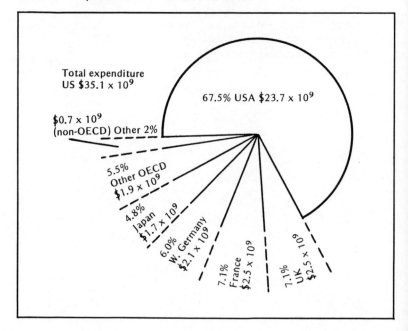

is concentrated in the USA and how the share of the non-OECD*
countries is minimal.

Although US expenditure dominates that of all other countries it
is pertinent to note that this is in part a reflection of the great
wealth of that country. *Figure 4* shows how the sums spent on R &
D in certain countries compare with the GNP's† of these countries.

**Figure 4   R & D expenditure as %
GNP, estimated for 1967**

**Figure 5   R & D expenditure by
objectives as % GNP - 1964**

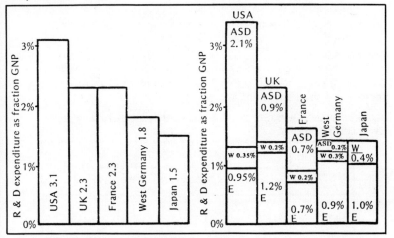

While in absolute terms US R & D expenditure far exceeds that
of other countries it is clear that this is the product of a slightly
larger fraction of a far larger GNP.

Not all of the world's R & D expenditure is directed towards
strictly economic goals. Much is spent on non-commercial activities
of prestige and security interest i.e. on defense, on space exploration
and on atomic energy. We can thus split R & D expenditure into
three broad categories. One will be this prestige/security category of
atomic, space and defense research (ASD); another the category of
economically motivated R & D (E); the third will include health and
welfare research and also generally non-directed basic research (W).
These categories account for varying percentages of GNP in different
countries, as is shown in *Figure 5.*

The fractions of national income spent on economic and welfare
research in the developed industrial OECD nations vary far less widely
than do the overall totals. This is clearly because of the wide

*The Organisation for Economic Cooperation and Development (OECD). Its
membership includes: the whole of Northern and Western Europe, USA,
Canada, Japan, Australia and New Zealand. The organisation thus represents
all the economically advanced capitalist countries.
†If you do not understand what GNP means see Appendix 2.

variation in spending in the atomic, space and defense sector. Notable is the high proportion of GNP allocated to this sector in the USA, which reflects not only that country's major defense commitment but the high level of expenditure on the Apollo space programme which was evident in the middle and late 1960s.

In turning now to examine the sources of funds and the institutions in which they are spent we will narrow our field of enquiry to the UK. The institutional sources of the funds spent on R & D can be divided into government, industry, and a category of 'others', which will include institutes of higher education (e.g. universities), and non-profit-making trusts, foundations and research organisations.

The performing sectors can again be divided into the same categories, and *Figure 6* shows how funds flow between the funding sectors and the performing sectors in the UK.

Figure 6   Flow of R & D finance between funding and performing sectors, UK £million, 1969—70

FUNDING SECTOR	PERFORMING SECTOR			TOTAL
	Govt.	*Industry*	*Other*	
Govt.	240.3	224.4	96.1	558.8
Industry	12.6	423.8	24.9	461.3
Other	9.8	34.8	17.7	61.8
Total	267.7	681.0	138.2	1081.9

The figure which dominates *Figure 6* is the sum of money which is spent *by* industry on research performed *within* industry   this accounted for almost 40% of UK R & D expenditure in 1969—70. Of total government spending in this same year, about 70% (half of which was performed in industry) had atomic, aerospace and defense objectives: of the remaining 30% only a small proportion, less than 3% of overall government R & D spending, was directly economic in its objectives.

In this book we wish to focus on some of the interesting and important problems which relate to R & D in private firms. We do not intend to deny the atomic, space and defense sector its economic importance; clearly any category of expenditure which accounts for up to 2% of GNP (as in the USA) is bound to be economically significant. What distinguishes this sector is that economic considerations are not of *paramount* importance in regulating the decisions which are made in the allocation of resources. This is not the case in the sector of activity that we have called economically oriented R & D — here we would expect to find economic consider-ations governing investment decisions and it is these decisions which are of most interest to us in this book.

Nevertheless, let us briefly examine some of the economic aspects of atomic, space and defense research.

We will first of all consider its *effects*. Research in this sector is not normally justified in terms of its contribution to economic growth.* Occasionally, space and defense research will lead to economic benefits — usually described as 'spin-off' benefits. These are rare, so invoking their existence as a *justification* for such expenditure is somewhat dishonest. The effects on economic growth of research expenditure in this sector are minimal.

Economic considerations can, on the face of it, be dismissed as explanations for atomic, space and defense research. In fact, considerations such as 'national prestige' and 'national security' have been seen as the driving force behind these massive expenditures. At one level of analysis this is of course true, but it is possible to go beyond such considerations to argue even an economic basis to these activities. Marxists argue, for example, that economic† considerations provide the basic direction for *all* human activity. War and the threat of war are used to preserve the economic positions of nation-states, both with respect to each other and in terms of preserving the economic interests of national ruling classes. To put it bluntly — war is necessary to sustain and to defend capitalism. It has also been argued by non-Marxist economists that massive expenditure on war and on space exploration, including research expenditure, is necessary to make capitalism function. Keynes, for example, argued that in order to preserve growth and employment it is necessary for governments to spend large sums of money over and above those they raise in taxes. War and space exploration provide useful outlets for such sums of money — by paying men to engage in activities which have no intrinsic economic worth, money flows into the economy and demand for the products of industry is kept high.

But we are not interested here in examining these explanations in detail. What we are concerned to point out is that research

---

*Research into the civil uses of atomic energy is the possible exception to this case — but even here we do not find economic considerations ruling the decision processes.

†By 'economic', Marxists mean those activities by which people produce those things they need to live; this is a much broader meaning of the word than that given to it by orthodox economists.

expenditure in the atomic, space and defense sectors need not necessarily be viewed as completely divorced from economic considerations.

To discuss the way in which economic growth is more directly related to research and development, and to look at the ways in which economic considerations govern the planning of this activity, we focus on R & D expenditure in the 'economically oriented' category.

Thus we can conclude that in the UK the *bulk of economically oriented research and development is funded by industry and performed within industry.* This sector of R & D expenditure is subject to the imperatives of a market economy, and we would expect the sorts of decision processes involved in research planning to reflect these imperatives. This book will go on to examine the ways in which such economic principles govern industry's involvement in research and development.

Questions

1. Which are the top ranking countries in terms of R & D expenditure? What are the approximate sizes of their budgets?
2. What is meant by 'economically oriented R & D' and how do the sums spent stand in relation to other quantities?
3. On what basis are we able to argue that most 'economically oriented R & D' in the UK is funded by private industry and performed by private industry?

Points for discussion or essays

1. In this chapter we concentrated on R & D spending in the western developed countries. It is well known that the gap between these and the underdeveloped countries of the 'Third World' is enormous. Details for discussion can be found in Sklair (1972), Chapter 1.

2. In the light of examples known to the reader what do you think of our statement that the spin-off benefits from atomic, space and defense research 'are rare, so invoking them as a *justification* for such expenditure is somewhat dishonest'?

Why should anybody have to invoke them as a justification for these expenditures?

Chapter Three
Research, Technology and Growth

Growths through R & D

Individual companies invest in research and development
because they believe that in the longer term they will be rewarded
with profits and/or growth. (See Chapter 4). A simplified linear
view of the processes assumed to follow from research is sketched in
Figure 7. It shows how benefits are assumed to accrue not only to
the firm but also to the national economy.

Figure 7   The linear view of the benefits of R & D

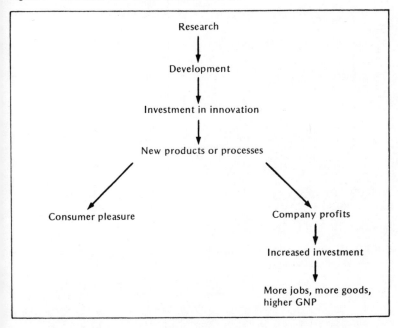

To view this as a linear process is to imply that each successive
step is the logical outcome of its predecessor. To feed in research at
the top is then to guarantee economic growth as an end-product. If
the processes were like this then R & D expenditure would be a
sufficient condition for economic growth.

The evidence suggests that this is far from the case. The economist
B.R. Williams compared the R & D expenditures of a number of

13

countries in the years 1950 to 1959 with the growth rate of these countries between 1955 and 1964. (The five year time lag being an estimate of the time it might take for economic benefits to result from research.) If research expenditure were a sufficient condition for growth we would expect to find a *correlation* between the two sets of figures i.e. although other factors might intrude, and although the choice of a five year time lag might not be appropriate, we would expect high research expenditure to tend to be associated with high rates of growth. As is evident from Williams' results, illustrated in *Figure 8*, no such correlation exists. Indeed there is a hint of a reverse relationship — lower rates of growth being associated with higher research expenditures! If the truth were as simple as this we would therefore achieve higher growth in the UK by *cutting back* on R & D expenditure!

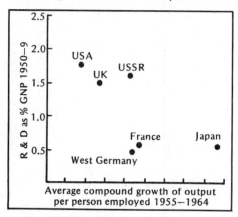

Figure 8   The relationship between R & D expenditure and economic growth. From Williams (1967)

There are, of course, reasons why these results cannot be taken at face value. For a start, much of the R & D expenditure of the big spenders (in *Figure 8*, UK, USA and USSR) is on defense and prestige research where an economic return is not anticipated. Also there is a considerable international availability of the results of R & D — technological knowhow is traded, and the results of scientific research are published freely. In addition, even if all research were to result in innovation the consequences in terms of economic growth would be different in different countries — mature industrial countries will be, as Williams writes 'somewhat in the position of Alice in the Garden of Flowers, where it took all the running to keep in the same place and faster than that to get anywhere'.

Despite these reservations, Williams' analysis does suggest that Britain, for example, is not getting all that it might out of the money invested in R & D. The view that Britain is good at invention but less good at taking economic advantage of it is one that is often heard, and supported by many anecdotes. The implication is that

R & D is doing its job but that somewhere down the linear chain that leads to growth something is going wrong. The error may be attributed to bad management or to a shortage of the sort of capital needed to take the inevitable risks involved in innovation.

Such explanations are less than satisfactory if the inherent weaknesses of the linear model are recognised. Recent studies, (typically: Langrish, Gibbons, Evans and Jevons, 1972), have emphasised the importance of what has been called 'need-pull' in the innovation process — innovation, it has been discovered, is rarely triggered off just by invention ('idea-push'), in the fashion suggested by the linear model. It appears that inventions, however beautiful and exciting and promising they seem to the inventor, are not going to be adopted by industry unless they meet industry's needs, and these needs are associated more closely with market forces than with technical ingenuity or sophistication.

In particular, it has been recognised that the contribution of *scientific knowledge* to industrial innovation is much less, or much less direct, than is implied by the linear model. As Jevons writes in *Wealth from Knowledge*, 'Perhaps science is not the father of technology but an anonymous well wisher who sends it gifts through the post'. We must beware of course of a problem of definition. Most of the research and development work done in industry is by no means 'science' in the sense of pure science in which the word is used by Jevons. In the figures used by Williams, applied research and development work preponderates heavily over basic research. What Williams' results seem to show is that even *applied* research and development does not lead directly to economic growth.

The specific problem of the nature of the innovation process, and in particular its relation to scientific knowledge, is not our concern in this book. In this chapter we have merely been concerned to outline the problems of relating research expenditure to its economic returns on a national scale.

Technology and growth

The immediate goal of most industrial R & D is technological innovation. By this means industry either produces goods which consumers prefer (or are deemed or persuaded to prefer), or produces goods more efficiently and at lower cost. The consequence of such increases in economic efficiency will be reflected, albeit imperfectly, in a higher Gross National Product. Thus technology contributes to growth.

But *how much* does technology contribute to growth? Growth can take place in the absence of technological progress if, to put it simply, factories are used to produce more factories and not just to produce goods for consumption. Growth will also occur if more people become engaged in industrial production. In these examples growth will result from in the first case an increase in the amount of capital in use, in the second place an increase in the amount of labor in use. Economists have traditionally assumed that a firm's output (or a nation's output), is a function of these two 'factors of production' — capital and labor.

We have seen in Chapter 1 that it is possible to express output in terms of a production function — as a function of capital and labor inputs, in the fashion of traditional economics. We have also seen that if we are to take account of technical change we must also include in our production function a variable which represents the types of techniques which are used.

Thus a more general expression of the production functions is

$$Q = f(K, L, T)$$

where K = capital, L = labor, and T = is a factor which depends on the state of technology, on the type of techniques available and in use.

SOLOW'S ANALYSIS

It is on the basis of this form of expression of the relationship between output and technology that the economist Robert Solow attempted to measure the contribution of technical change to growth in the USA. For a full account see Rosenberg (1971).

Essentially, Solow's method consisted of the fitting of a particular form of the production function to data on inputs and outputs in the USA economy between 1909 and 1949. Solow expressed the state of technique as the multiplier $(A(t))$ in the production function:
$Q = A(t) f(K, L)$

His conclusion was that while output per man *doubled* in the period 1909 to 1949 only 12½% of this increase was attributable to the use of more capital. 87½% of the increase was therefore attributable to something else — Solow called it 'technical progress' (not to be confused with 'technical change').

We may or may not be surprised by this result. It is likely to be subject to a wide margin of error due largely to the problems in data collection. It is also likely to be considerably biased towards the high side for at least two reasons:
1. By virtue of Solow's definition of *technical progress*, since by writing $Q = A(t) f(K, L)$ it is implied that all changes in output which are not due to changes in K and L are due to changes in A. Thus Solow's *technical progress* is a *residual* which includes not only what we would normally mean by advances in technological knowhow but also such things as a better and more healthy workforce, and the effects of growing markets.

2. Solow assumes that technical change is *disembodied*, i.e. he supposes that new techniques can be applied to already existing capital equipment as well as being incorporated in new equipment — technical progress is assumed not to require the expenditure of capital. It is a consequence of the method of analysis used that this assumption leads to an underestimation of the contribution of investment to growth.

DENISON'S ANALYSIS

A similar but more comprehensive and, in many ways, more sophisticated exercise was performed by Denison (1968). In his analysis, technical progress still emerges as a *residual* factor but whereas in the Solow analysis it is residual after the effects of capital and labor, in Denison's analysis technical progress is residual after a much more comprehensive range of factors. As a consequence, as we might expect, the effect of 'technical progress' is seen to be much smaller.

Denison's results for the UK are discussed below. His analysis was based on data for the years 1950—62. During this time national income rose at an annual rate of 2.29%. Denison's analysis breaks this figure of 2.29 down into components as illustrated in *Table 1*. His residual attempts to exclude factors such as those suggested in the discussion on Solow. Thus Denison's labor inputs are not just the numerical totals of those employed but attempt to incorporate the effect of education; the economies of scale due, for example, to increased markets are specifically estimated and subtracted from the residual, as are estimates of the effect of improved resource allocations etc. Denison described his residual factor as 'advances in knowledge'.

We would expect this new, smaller, residual to be more representative of our common-language idea of 'technical progress'. It is now seen to be responsible for about 1/3rd (in fact 33.2%) of the UK's growth — which seems to be a more reasonable estimate than the 87½% contribution derived by Solow for the USA. But the figure is still subject, of course, to a wide margin of error being influenced not just by problems of the collection of input/output data but by the interpretation and calculations based on these data — to attribute for example 0.29 percentage points to the effect of education is necessarily to make assumptions which are at the very least contentious.

Some conclusions on research, technology and growth

It is clear from the work of Williams that we do not find, and indeed should not expect to find, a simple relationship between research expenditure and economic growth on a national scale.

We have seen that economists have attempted to gauge the

Table 1   Summary of Denison's analysis of UK Growth Rate 1950—62 adapted from Denison (1968) p. 314.

UK Growth Rate:	Breaks down into:	Breaks down into:
2.29% annual growth between 1950 and 1962	1.11 due to increased inputs	0.6 due to increased inputs of labor (0.29 of which due to education)
		0.51 due to increased inputs of capital
		1.11
	1.18 therefore due to increased output per unit input	0.03 due to more efficient use of old knowledge
		0.12 due to improved allocation of resources
		0.36 due to economies of scale
		−0.09 due to irregularities in demand
		0.42 subtotal
		0.76 therefore the residual, assumed due to advances in knowledge
	2.29	1.18

contribution of technological advances to economic growth, and their methods have usually depended on listing all the *other* things which contribute to growth and which are quantifiable, examining the relations between output and these inputs over a period of time, and attributing the residual — the growth which cannot be explained by means of their list — to technical progress. Solow's list was capital and labor, and his residual came out at 87½% (USA). Denison's list was more complex and his residual was much lower, at 33% (UK).* Such results are clearly dependent on the form of analysis used — both in the sense suggested above (the scope of the list) and the precise way in which the meaning of the question 'what is the contribution of technology to economic growth?' is interpreted. Differences in interpretation of this question are hidden in the forms of production function used and it is not our purpose or intent to attempt the complex analysis which will make them explicit.

Moreover, the problems of measurement and the uncertainties

---

*Denison's estimate for the USA was 23%.

associated with the quantities measured make the precise numerical results of little significance; the analyses of Denison and Solow therefore seem to have limited meaning. But what they do tell us is that economic growth cannot be explained completely unless some account is taken of an increase in technical production efficiency, which can only be attributed to technology. If we note that indices of national income do not incorporate a measure of the changing *nature* of goods produced — a product with a higher use-value but which sells for the same price does not add to GNP — we might attribute to technology an even greater contribution to material well being than that suggested by the analyses of income growth. We can conclude with some confidence that technology plays an important role in increasing the output and changing the nature of industrial goods.

Questions

1. What is meant by the linear model of innovation?

2. What are the cited results of B.R. Williams, and why cannot they be taken at face value?

3. What is meant, in the context of this section, by 'residual analysis'?

4. Why are the results of such analyses subject to a wide margin of error?

5. How does Denison's analysis differ from that of Solow?

Points for discussions or essays

1. Some people are arguing today that the effects of economic growth in the advanced countries have been so catastrophic on the environment and on the social fabric of those countries that growth should cease to be the primary aim of economic policy. If we accept this proposal does this mean that technological change and therefore R & D activities will have to cease? What objectives could R & D be called to serve in a no-growth economy?

2. Discuss the statement that 'Perhaps science is not the father of technology but an anonymous well-wisher who sends it gifts through the post'.

3. Solow calls his residual 'technical progress'. How does this term differ from that of 'technical change'?

4. In the light of what we say in this section draw up a flow-chart similar to that of *Figure* 7 which more accurately shows the benefits that accrue from R & D.

Chapter Four
Research and Development in British Industry

In the year ending April, 1970 British industry, public and private, spent over £700 million on scientific and technological research and development. This figure includes money which industry financed from its own funds, for R & D to be carried out in its own establishments or in universities or research associations, and money which industry received from other institutions, particularly the British government, in the way of grants or contracts. Altogether almost one-third of the money which, in one way or another, industry 'handled' in its R & D activities was provided by the Government (£224 million to be precise), with another twentieth (£33 million) coming from overseas sources (either foreign governments or firms). Such figures however, apart from showing the extent to which the government contributes to research and development in industry, rather than just to those research establishments immediately concerned with government prerogatives (like the Atomic Energy Authority or defense establishments), do not give any indication of the spread of expenditure over various industries.

R & D expenditure represents about 2% of the total turnover of British industry; that is, about 4½% of the total net output*. Yet it is a commonly held belief that advanced industries, such as the aircraft industry, must spend much more on R & D, compared to the industry's turnover, than a technically 'backward' industry such as clothing and footwear. So what *are* the differences in spending between different industries and, more importantly, *why* are there these differences?

Inter-industry differences in R & D spending

The official statistics of R & D expenditure divide industry into forty 'product groups'. Full details of how much each product group spends on R & D and where the money comes from can be obtained from Central Statistical Office's publication 'Research and Development Expenditure' HMSO (1973) but there is no need to reproduce

---

Turnover is the total of all sales of goods produced and work done. Obviously in calculating it for the whole of industry the turnover of some industries is counted twice, as those industries' products are inputs to other industries. *Net output* is the turnover less the cost of purchases of materials and fuel.

their tables in full here. The main features are presented in the diagrams below. (*Figures 9—11*) The first thing to be noticed here, as has already been mentioned in the last chapter, is the unequal distribution of government funds. In fact, almost exactly seven-eighths of goverment contributions goes to only *two* product groups

Figure 9   R & D expenditures in British industry — all sources of finance.
Figure 10   R & D expenditure in British industry — financed by private industry itself. Figure 11   R & D expenditure in British industry — financed by the Government

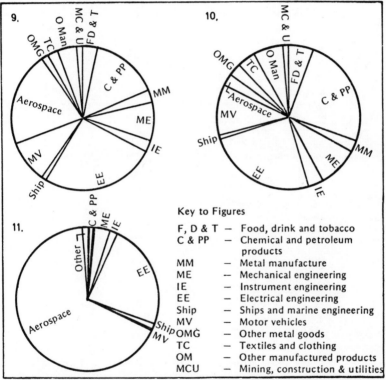

Key to Figures

F, D & T	—	Food, drink and tobacco
C & PP	—	Chemical and petroleum products
MM	—	Metal manufacture
ME	—	Mechanical engineering
IE	—	Instrument engineering
EE	—	Electrical engineering
Ship	—	Ships and marine engineering
MV	—	Motor vehicles
OMG	—	Other metal goods
TC	—	Textiles and clothing
OM	—	Other manufactured products
MCU	—	Mining, construction & utilities

Note The figures show the distribution of R & D spending in 13 industrial groupings, for 1969—70.

— 'aerospace' (67% of total government contributions to industrial R & D) and 'electronic components and telecommunications' (20%)†. This situation obviously reflects the British government's concern.

†this product group is one of those included in the 'electrical engineering' group in the figures below.

The cost of developing the advanced technology involved in the manufacture of aeroplanes, communication, satellites and electronic apparatus is so high that private companies are either unable or unwilling to take the risks involved. Therefore, the government, if it wishes to preserve or build up indigenous expertise in these areas to maintain some kind of defense capability or to be able to get British industry a share of the international aerospace and electronic equipment markets, must provide the money for the necessary R & D to be carried out.

Although only seven product groups altogether (including aerospace and electronics) receive more than 1% each of the total government contribution to industrial R & D, for many a product group the government contribution is an important percentage of that product group's total R & D expenditure. *Table 2* gives an indication of this.

Table 2   % government contribution to product group's R & D in 1969—70.

Product group	%
Aerospace	89
Ships and marine engines	59
Electronic components inc. telecommunications	37.5
Electronic computers	25
Industrial plant and steelwork	21.5
Scientific instruments	19
General mechanical engineering	15
Railway equipment	14
Leather and fur	14

The money that government contributes to the various product group's R & D expenditure is not the same from year to year of course. For example, the railway equipment product group, shown on *Table 1* as receiving 14% of its R & D spending from Government sources in 1969—70 (equivalent to £355 000) last received any money in 1967—8, and then only £3000! And, given the general low level of spending by such industries, then government contributions (usually for special purposes) show up as a large percentage of the total.

The second thing to be noticed from statistics on expenditure by industry is the great disparity in R & D spending between the different product groups, varying from £171 million for aerospace down to £367 000 in 'leather and fur'. But without some knowledge of the relative sizes of the particular industries involved such figures have limited use if we are trying to detect general reasons for spending differences. Hence it is usual to compare the R & D expenditure figure for a particular product group with that group's net output. The comparison is usually expressed in the form: *R & D expenditure from all sources, as a percentage of net output.* This is called the *research intensity* or *R & D intensity*. *Table 3* gives a selection of research intensities for different product groups.

Table 3   R & D intensities — a selection of British product groups

Category	R & D intensity (R & D expenditure as % of net output)	Sample product groups (R & D intensity in brackets)
1. Very intensive	10	Aerospace (35.8)
2. High	4—10	Plastics (7.2): scientific instruments (5.8): motor vehicles (4.7)
3. Medium	2—4	Pottery and glass (3.5): textile machinery (2.4): general electrical engineering (2.2)
4. Low	1—2	Rubber (1.8): iron and steel (1.3): food, drink, and tobacco (1.2)
5. Negligible	<1	Paper, printing and publishing (0.5): clothing and footwear (0.2): construction (0.1)

Note: The research intensities were calculated from R & D expenditure figures for 1969—70 and net output figures for 1968.

The product groups are categorised by their research intensities. Categories 1 and 2 contain those industries in which research and development is one of the most vital aspects of company operations — the product groups here are usually said to be 'research-based' or 'science-based'.

In categories 4 and 5 R & D does not have the same central importance. These product groups are not characterised by continuous and rapid technological change in the same way as those in categories 1 and 2, though large sums of money may be spent on non-technological product development, like market research.

There is no need to memorise the detailed figures which have been presented above. The essential point which must be grasped is that some industries (or product groups) lay out and use up much more money on scientific and technological research than others. In general, in the USA as well as in the UK, the aerospace, electrical and mechanical engineering, chemical, electronics and scientific instrument industries account for the largest proportion of industrial research and development expenditure, have the highest research intensities and receive, both absolutely and relatively, the highest proportion of government contributions to industrial R & D. But why should this be? The rest of this chapter sets out to answer this question.

The Reasons for inter-industry difference

Before we can answer the question just posed it is necessary to discuss briefly why firms (and therefore industries) spend *any money at all* on research and development. As a general rule, the force governing the activities of firms in capitalist economies is the maximisation of profits, though there may be many other factors which constrain this process at various times. Research and development, as one of the activities of a firm, must be seen in this context. Essentially any firm engaging in research activities is trying to achieve one of two things — either (1) to 'discover' or 'invent' some new *product* (or modify an old or existing product) or (2) to 'discover' or 'invent' some new way of making its existing products; that is, some new *process* or modification of an existing process. Now, obviously, if a firm manages to invent a completely new product the manufacture of this product may involve changes in production methods. Such changes may be major — for example, the installation of completely new machinery or the drastic re-organisation of existing machinery and work methods or the devising of a new process to deal (say) with previously unused raw materials — or they may be very small indeed involving perhaps no more than (say) a slight change in the temperature at which one of the processes had to operate. Thus it is not always possible to separate the introduction of a new product from the introduction of the process which accompanies it. However, there will be many modifications to machines or alterations in production methods which will not be associated with the introduction of a new product. The invention and introduction into production of new products is essential to the firm. If it is particularly subject to market forces, being one firm amongst many competitors in its field of operations, then it must often review the products it offers. It is always possible that some other firm will come up with a new product which is so popular in the market that demand for other firms' competing products will decrease. As a result, those firms which do not devote adequate resources to developing new products or modifying existing products to improve their performance or extend their range of applications will in the longer term be squeezed out of the market, will suffer a reduction in profits and may go out of business.

Even in those sectors of the economy where market forces have less influence, where firms are very large and have few domestic competitors, research into new products is still important. To begin with, these firms, large though they are in the national context, have equally large, if not larger, *international* competitors. It is particularly significant therefore, that industries which have firms which engage in activities on an international scale have high research intensities (aerospace, electronics, chemicals, electrical engineering). And even if *domestic* competition is not great it still exists. In addition, in those industries which come more into contact with individual consumers (like food and clothing or detergents) there is a need for new product research to stimulate appetites so as to keep the general level of consumption, and therefore sales and profits, high. The large number of 'new', 'improved' products which regale our senses on TV and posters may largely be a result of the effects of advertising men and designers but there is an element of research and development in them as well.

Even those economists who do not see profit maximisation as the principal driving force at work in large corporations accord research and development a key place, as a means by which the firm does achieve its goals. Galbraith (1974), who considers that it is the drive for survival and *growth* of the corporation by the group of planners and managers who now run firms (Galbraith calls them the techno-structure), states:

> 'Associated with growth, as a goal of the technostructure, is technological virtuosity. . . . . Capacity for expansion . . . . . . depends very largely on capacity for innovation. It is by technical innovation, real or simulated, that the firm holds and recruits customers for its existing products and expands to produce new ones. Such capacity for innovation is obviously important for keeping or expanding the firm's share of weapons, space and other businesses with technological dynamic'.

And 'technical innovation' is only possible if the firm devotes a large amount of resources to scientific and technological research and development work. The rationale for research into new methods of production is similar to that for new products. It is continually necessary for the price of goods produced to be kept down and in fact to be reduced as much as possible. Given a certain constancy in the level of wages there are a number of ways that costs of production can be reduced — reductions in the cost of raw materials and machines, more efficient use of resources (e.g. reduction of wastage, reorganisation of factory), and introduction of machines which reduce the requirement for labour, are the three most important methods. Such reductions can only be accomplished by research and development which will actually result in new machines or improvements in existing ones.

The view that firms (and, therefore, industries) devote resources (spend money on equipment, hire scientists and technologists) to research and development to produce new products or processes (technical innovations) has so far only been baldly stated. What evidence is there that industries who 'do' a great deal of R & D get more benefit from it than do those who do little? The following reading summarises a number of studies which British and American economists have made to establish the connection, if any, between research and development expenditures and one measure of benefit, the increase in output per worker employed (called productivity).

From Norris and Vaizey (1973) Chapter 10.

Research and development expenditures and productivity change

Innovations are made in order to produce new products, to modify existing products, or to make existing products in more efficient ways. As research and development expenditures are made by firms with the ultimate aim of producing an innovation, it follows that we might expect to see some systematic relationship between research and development expenditure and productivity growth, a relationship that would vary from industry to industry.

It is not easy to test this hypothesis for the UK over a long period as the earliest year for which research and development expenditures by industry are available is 1961. The time lags between expenditure and results are long and variable, as we have seen, and it is not clear which periods of productivity growth should be used to trace cause and effect. Since about 1970, too, it seems that significant productivity growth has occurred because of changes in the manpower policies followed by firms. In what follows we compare research and development expenditure, for 1961, as a percentage of net output in that year with the growth of output per man over the period 1963–70.

The unemployment rate in these years was 2.6% and 3.4%, respectively, which is about as close as it is possible to get without drastically shortening the time period. Thus, to some extent, the two years were similar in the main, known, short term factor affecting productivity per man, the state of trade. The comparison is confined to manufacturing industry as private research and development activity outside manufacturing is negligible and there is, in any case, no available breakdown of such expenditure. The degree of aggregation is dictated by the research and development statistics. The results are presented in *Table 4*.

If we leave aside the aircraft industry for the moment, we can see that productivity in the research intensive industries increased faster than it did in the other manufacturing industries. The two groups of industries (food, and timber and paper) with

Table 4   Research intensity and the rate of growth of output per man in UK manufacturing industry, 1963—70.

	R & D expenditure as a percentage of net output (1961)	Annual percentage rate of growth of output per man (1963—70)
Food, drink and tobacco	0.8	1.9
Chemicals	6.7	6.2
Metal manufacture	1.3	2.0
Mechanical engineering, metal goods not elsewhere specified, shipbuilding	2.4	2.8
Electronics and telecommunications	18.6	6.3
Other electrical goods	9.0	5.3
Motor vehicles and railways	4.1	3.0
Aircraft	54.1	2.2
Textiles, leather and clothing	1.0	3.8
Bricks	1.4	3.3
Timber and paper	0.4	1.9
Other manufacturing	2.6	3.9

Sources: *Statistics of Science and Technology*, London, HMSO (1967). *National Income and Expenditure*, London, HMSO (1970). *Department of Employment Gazette*, London, HMSO (1972). *Monthly Digest of Statistics*, Central Statistical Office (1972).

the lowest research intensity, had the lowest rate of productivity growth. The odd man out is aircraft, with a very high research intensity and below average producitvity growth. Expenditure on research and development in this industry is largely financed by the government and non-economic considerations probably dominate. In what follows we omit the aircraft industry.

There was a statistical association between research intensity and producitivity growth between 1963—70. This does not of course, indicate a causal relationship. There are some theoretical grounds for expecting a causal link between research and development expenditures and productivity growth, but there are equally some reasons why we find it odd that such a relationship should be observable.

First, a significant proportion of research and development expenditures are devoted to the introduction of new products, and it is well known that conventional measures of output fail to capture the full impact of new products. More precisely, it has been argued that as new products are often introduced at higher relative prices than they sell for in the long run, and as price indices tend to underrepresent new products, two biases will occur. First, the price indices will be biased upwards and hence real output will be biased downwards. Secondly, as prices of new products fall, and as they are increasingly reflected in

27

price indices, an impression of producitivity change is given when there is none.

A second reason for expecting no close statistical relationship between research and development expenditures and productivity change is that the system of national income accounting fails to allow for quality change, and much research and development is aimed at improving the quality of products. Thus, when price increases are due in part to quality change, the price indices will in some sense be biased upwards and, correspondingly, real output and productivity change will be biased downwards.

Thirdly, we have already seen that many industries can improve their productivity through improvements in the intermediate goods they purchase. Much of the effect of research and development expenditure in the engineering industries, for example, will be felt as an improvement in the productivity of the user industries. Correlating research and development expenditures with productivity change in the same industry misses this inter-industry effect.

Fourthly, we have already emphasised that, to have any effect on output, much research and development must be embodied in plant and machinery . . . . Differences in the speed with which embodiment occurs is a special case of a more general proposition, which states that the effects of innovation on productivity depend essentially on the extent to which, and the speed at which, the innovation is diffused. Thus, the whole complex of factors (connected with the concept of) diffusion comes into play.

For these reasons, the fit observed in *Table 4* seems too good to be true. Sargent has also looked at the association between research intensity and productivity growth. He used the density of employment of qualified scientists and engineers (QSE), instead of research and development expenditures, as his measure of research activity, and he used total factor productivity* instead of labor productivity. Sargent found no correlation between productivity and the QSE density by industry, in the two time periods he studied, 1955—60 and 1960—64. When only the science based industries were included in the sample, however, QSE density explained about one-half of the variance in total factor productivity.

A study in the USA has, however, produced more positive results. Minasian tested the hypothesis that 'productivity

---

*Total factor productivity is a measure of output in relation to all factors of production, not just labor.

increases are associated with investment in the improvement of technology and the greater the expenditures for research and development the greater the rate of growth of productivity'. He tested this hypothesis by using data on firms — eighteen firms in the chemicals industry and five drugs firms — over the period 1947—57. Obviously, this is more meaningful than our broad industrial categories. The productivity measure used was total factor productivity derived from a Cobb-Douglas production function†. Surprisingly, high correlation coefficients of around 0.7 were obtained, and, interestingly enough, various other hypotheses (notably that productivity would be explained by gross investment) were apparently disproved. As the author points out, however, this was a strictly non-random sample and the results should not be generalized without further thought. There are good grounds for arguing that the chemical industry is, in this respect, not typical of industry as a whole.

Attempts to relate productivity growth with research and development expenditures seem to be very sensitive to the precise forms of the two variables that are used, the time period and the industrial breakdown, and to the industrial coverage that is used.

It seems therefore that, from the results presented in this reading, there is some relationship between spending on research and development and growth in productivity. But what exactly are the links in the chain connecting these two things? The main link is covered by the concept of 'technological change' which, it seems obvious to suggest, must be a result of R & D activities. The next question then is — to what extent is productivity growth a result of technological change? The most elaborate analysis of this question has been carried out by the British economist W.E.G. Salter (1960).

Salter collected data on 28 British industries for the years 1924—50. From that data he was able to calculate the increase in productivity (measured as output per head) over that period, for each industry. His results are shown in *Table 5*.

The median increase in productivity in this period was about 50%, though, as you can see, there were variations — from an increase of over 200% on the one hand (for cutlery and electricity generation) to a *decline* of 16% on the other (for the wallpaper industry). Obviously it is impossible to give a full explanation of the range of productivity changes observed. For example, why should productivity of the 'hosiery and knitted goods' industry have increased by a half

†A Cobb-Douglas production function has the form $Q = A K\alpha L^{1-\alpha}$ where A and α are constants.

Table 5 Changes in output and output per head over the period 1924—50 for selected UK industries. (NB. The industry names are different from those in other tables, due to different systems of classification).

Industry ranked according to increase in productivity	% increase in output (1950 over 1924)	Increase in output/head (1950 as % of increase of 1924)
1. Cutlery	334	212
2. Electricity generation	994	211
3. Rubber manufactures	468	194
4. Steel tubes	302	140
5. Cement	176	139
6. Glass	269	111
7. Cocoa and confectionery	71	99
8. Chemicals	428	94
9. Spirit distilling	101	91
10. Wire and wire working	154	78
11. Paper and board	139	73
12. Matches	24	56
13. Linoleum	76	54
14. Hosiery and knitted goods	83	53
15. Brushes and brooms	97	51
16. Tinplate	−14	44
17. Brick and fireclay	58	42
18. Iron and steel	98	40
19. Coke ovens	37	37
20. Jute	−35	34
21. Cotton spinning	−17	29
22. Paint and varnish	127	28
23. Boots and shoes	12	25
24. Blast furnaces	27	22
25. Coal mining	−27	20
26. Leather	25	11
27. Brewing	− 3	− 9
28. Wallpaper	−28	−16

while that of the 'boot and shoe' industry only increased by a quarter?

Salter is then concerned with the relationship between changes in labor productivity (output per head) and other variables in the industries (e.g. labor costs, material costs, output and prices). He states:

'The analysis of the industry data suggests that uneven rates of productivity growth are closely associated with the main features of the inter-industry pattern of growth. Industries which have achieved substantial increases in output per head have, in general, been successful in other respects: their costs have risen the least, the relative prices of their products has fallen, output has expanded greatly, and in most cases employment has increased by more than the average. On the other hand, industries with small increases in output per head are generally declining industries — at least in relative terms. Their costs and selling prices have risen the most, output has increased much less than average (or even fallen), and increases in employment are below average.' (p. 124)

Salter goes on to assess on the basis of his analysis three alternative hypotheses which might account for the observed labor productivity changes — increased labor efficiency, factor substitution and improvements in technology.

He rejects his *first* hypothesis — that increased labor productivity is due to increases in the 'personal efficiency of labor' (in other words, workers working harder) — on the grounds that such increases should be spread fairly evenly over all industries. They are not, and it is difficult to see how workers might, say, treble their skill, effort and intelligence in some industries and halve it in others.

The *second* hypothesis is that the increase in labour productivity is due to 'factor substitution', specifically 'the substitution of labor by capital'. This assumes a certain constant *set* of techniques (see Chapter 1), each member of the set needing different amounts of capital and labor to produce outputs. As labor (say) becomes more expensive in a particular firm, then that firm chooses, from the set, another technique more sparing with labor. In other words, increases in labor productivity would be the result of *technical* rather than of *technological* change. However, this hypothesis is also rejected though on grounds too complicated to be expounded here.

Salter's *third* hypothesis, the one he eventually *accepts*, is that the differences in productivity growth are due to differing rates of technological change between industries, differing rates of the *shift* of the production function (see p. 4).

He singles out two things which make up the rate of technological change. Firstly there are advances in scientific and technological knowledge ('improved techniques'). Obviously those industries which are relatively 'young', based on relatively new scientific and technological knowledge (such as electricity generation, rubber and chemicals in Salter's industry list), will have many things to discover, many avenues to explore; thus they will be responsible for the invention of many more products and techniques for making them. They will, therefore, be advancing technologically at a much greater rate than those industries which are more traditional in nature and where few technical developments are actually possible (like the brewing or wallpaper industries). The second factor is closely tied with the first. New techniques or products do not just happen. They have to be concretised in machinery, in a specific organisation of production; in short, they have to be *embodied* in capital equipment. Therefore those industries, it would be reasonable to assume, where such 'embodiment' was 'easier' would also be those where productivity increases due to newer techniques were also being realised. It is clear that those industries which are 'young', apart from being places of rapid technological advance, are also those which are just beginning to explore the possibilities of economies of scale and are therefore more ready and able to demand and introduce new techniques. More traditional industries have, within the technological possibilities of their day, reached the limit of such economies and are therefore not in the best position to introduce new techniques. New techniques and the seeking of economies of scale, therefore, go together. Of course the pursuit and realisation of economies of scale are not automatic activities. They depend on the availability of money for investment and this in turn depends on broader questions of the state of the economy and the demand for industry's products.

Near the end of his study, Salter commented, 'We should be entitled to much more confidence in the result if they could be confirmed by another set of observations based upon a different sample of industries operating in different circumstances'. W. B. Reddaway has provided this sample by examining similar statistics to Salter's but for a different time period — 1954—63 to be exact. Over

Table 7   Comparison of ranking order of 23 industries for movements, over the period 1924—50 and 1954—63, in output per head and in output

| | Ranking order | | | |
| | Output per head | | Output | |
	1924—50	1954—63	1924—50	1954—63
Electricity	2	1	1	1
Chemicals	8	2	3	2
Hosiery/knitted goods	12	3	13	5
Footwear	20	4	19	13
Glass	6	5	6	3
Paint	19	6	10	11
Cotton spinning	18	7	21	23
Bricks and fireclay	14	8	16	15
Leather	22	9	18	22
Wire	9	10	8	7
Brushes/brooms	13	11	12	19
Rubber	3	12	2	8
Paper/board	10	13	9	4
Linoleum	11	14	14	6
Jute	17	15	23	17
Coal-mining	21	16	22	20
Brewing	23	17	20	10
Cutlery	1	18	4	16
Iron and steel	15	19	11	14
Steel tubes	4	20	5	9
Cement	5	21	7	12
Cocoa/confectionery	7	22	15	18
Coke ovens	16	23	17	21

that period, productivity increased at an even faster rate than it did in the period 1924–50; the median output per head for Salter's figures showed an annual rate increase of 1.60% while for the 1954–63 period the figure was 1.84%. In general, Reddaway's analysis confirmed the points made in Salter's study. However, there were some interesting differences which will lead us to some concluding points on this connection between R & D spending and increases in productivity.

Table 7 compares the 1954–63 period with the 1924–50 period by *ranking* 23 industries in order of increases in output per head. Only 23 industries are compared because Reddaway could not repeat Salter's analysis over the whole range of industries.

Reddaway comments on this table as follows:—

'It will be seen that for output, there is a broad similarity in the ranking order. Only one industry — cutlery — shows a difference of more than nine places, which is about the average movement to be expected if there is no correlation between the rankings; one can *broadly* say that fast-growing industries in the earlier period continued to grow fast, declining or slow-growing industries continued to fare badly.

In terms of *output per head*, however, the short answer is that the correlation coefficient between the two rankings is negligible . . . . There are . . . far more exceptions than there were in the case of output to any generalisation that the previous period's star performers remain stars, and the laggards remain laggards'.
(W.B. Reddaway, Addendum W.E.G. Salter, 1966).

Let us look at the change in rankings of productivity increase in more detail.

Nine of the industries continued their productivity increase, in that their rank in the 1924–50 figures is similar (no more than 5 places higher or lower) to the 1954–63 figures: viz. electricity generation, glass, coal-mining, wire, brushes and brooms, paper and board, linoleum, jute, iron and steel. Eight considerably increased in rank: viz. chemicals, hosiery and knitwear, footwear, paint, cotton spinning, bricks and fireclay, leather, brewing. Six considerably decreased in rank: viz. rubber, cutlery, steel tubes, cement, cocoa and confectionery, coke ovens.

Now not too much should be made of these changes. Some of them are very puzzling indeed (eg. cutlery's drop from 1st to 18th place). However, it is particularly striking that those industries increasing their rank are principally those which sell their products direct to the public — *consumer* industries. And it is just these industries which have shown considerable growth since the Second World War in the period of increasing standard of living and rapidly expanding markets for consumer goods. Such a period of expansion, of course, is an ideal opportunity for making economies of scale and, in doing so, introducing completely new techniques, thus increasing productivity. In fact as Reddaway shows, there is a definite correlation between changes in output and changes in output per head — the larger the rises in output then the larger the rises in output per head.

To sum up Salter's and Reddaway's analyses — the explanation of the increases in productivity of British industry since the 1920s involves the following reasoning: the advances in scientific and technological knowledge led to new products and techniques being potentially available; in those industries which were recently founded, the 'fund' of knowledge was likely to be larger and it was just these industries which, by being 'younger', were able, in expanding, to take advantage of scale economies by employing new techniques. Older industries, expanding at a slower rate and having fewer technological avenues to explore, were thus less able to increase productivity. We can thus see why there is more technological innovation (and thus productivity increase) in some industries than in others.

The question we set out to answer was, why are there marked differences in *spending on R & D* between the various British industries? How does the analysis of the last few pages help to answer this?

It should be clear that the 'young' industries have so many opportunities in expanding to make increases in productivity and sell completely new products that they must spend much more on R & D if they are to get the necessary technical knowledge. 'Young' industries should thus be industries of high research intensity. But not all rapidly expanding industries will spend a lot on research and development. Their expansion may come merely from an increase in demand for products which are, relatively, technically unsophisticated. However, these industries (eg. food, drink, tobacco) can still ensure large increases in productivity by using new machines or materials developed in those sectors of the economy engaged in the manufacture of production goods (machines, raw materials). Thus one would expect high research intensities for these capital goods industries as they seek to discover and invent new processes and machinery to provide the rapidly expanding consumer goods industries with the equipment they are demanding.

In conclusion therefore, we can draw up a list of factors which account for the difference in research intensities between industries.

An industry will, in general, have a high research intensity if it fits into one or more of the following categories:
1. Those involved in work considered to be of vital national importance by the state (eg. aerospace, telecommunications).
2. Those industries which are relatively newly founded and can take

advantage of economies of scale and the wide range of scientific and technological opportunities that are available to them ('science-based' or 'research-based' industries, like plastics or oil refining).

3. Those industries supplying machinery or raw materials to support a rapidly expanding demand for products of consumer goods industries (eg. chemicals, electrical machinery).

Conversely, industries with low research intensities generally have little relevance to state needs, are concerned with production of consumer goods and (or) are relatively taditional with little chance of there being many new ideas to find.

In general, then, it can be said that research spending differences between industries is mainly due to technological factors, though this must not be stretched too far. High spending by governments on aircraft or space developments is not due to some inevitable, unstoppable drive of aircraft and space technology itself; it is a result of a *political* decision that those are the areas on which the governments choose (or are persuaded) to spend. Competition, also, has a role to play, though, as Norris and Vaizey put it, it is more important in 'determining the direction of inventive and innovative activity *within* an industry or firm' rather than in determining differences *between* industries.

Questions

1. List those product groups which figure in the various categories of research intensity? What typical research intensities do they exhibit.

2. Why do firms do R & D?

3. What are attempts to correlate research intensity with productivity changes designed to demonstrate? What results have been obtained?

4. Summarise the reasoning which establishes 'improvements in technology' as a reasonable explanation for productivity increases.

Points for discussion or essays

1. The table below gives 1968/9 figures for output and R & D expenditure for 5 out of the 8 industries listed below. Establish systematically what industries A, B, C, D and E might be.

List of industries: aerospace, clothing, footwear and leather; electronics and telecommunications; food, drink and tobacco; general electrical engineering; motor vehicles; scientific instruments; ships and marine engineering.

Industry	Net output (£m)	R & D expenditure as % of output	% of R & D by government
A	1100	4.2	3.2
B	620	20	40
C	550	0.2	negligible
D	325	3.9	7.1
E	300	0.8	30

This table gives 1968/9 figures for output and R & D expenditure for 5 out of the 8 industries listed below.

Chapter Five
Research and Development
in the Firm

There are many things which could be examined regarding the carrying out of research and development activities in individual firms. The easiest way to bring out the questions and problems is to study the policies of particular firms and the opinions of those firms' managers. So, below are reproduced two articles from the *New Scientist* magazine which gives an account of the R & D policies of two companies — the General Electric Company and Philips Gloeilampenfabriken.

Both these firms — one British, the other Dutch — have extensive interests in the field of electrical and electronic engineering and they figure amongst the largest such companies in the world, as *Table 8* shows.

GEC, with sales of nearly £1000 million, is the 9th largest private company in Britain. Its home labor force of 170,000 (in 1973) makes it Britain's largest private employer, with only the publicly-owned Post Office, National Coal Board, British Rail and British Steel Corporation employing more. GEC concerns itself with virtually everything which has some electrical association — from the installation of electricity generating equipment in power stations, through the

Table 8   The world's largest electrical/electronic engineering companies

Firm		Base country	turnover (1972) £m.
1.	General Electric*	USA	3961
2.	International Telephone & Telegraph	USA	3688
3.	Philips	Netherlands	2647
4.	Western Electric	USA	2534
5.	Siemens	West Germany	2017
6.	Westinghouse Electric	USA	1968
7.	Montedison	Italy	1562
8.	RCA	USA	1485
9.	AEG-Telefunken	West Germany	1338
10.	Hitachi	Japan	1238
11.	Matsushita Electrical Industries	Japan	1229
12.	GEC	UK	975

Figures from *The Times 1000, 1973–4*, Times Newspaper (1973)

*The US firm General Electric (GE) has no connections with the British General Electric Company (GEC).

manufacture of electric motors and domestic appliances to the production of wire and light bulbs. It also has involvement in the manufacture of aircraft, computers and nuclear reactors. Broadly, about 53% of the company's sales comes from electronic equipment (telecommunications and automation equipment, electronic components, cables and wire), 18% from heavy engineering, 15% from light engineering and 14% from consumer products (like 'Hotpoint' fridges and 'Morphy-Richards' hair-dryers). GEC is a giant in its various markets. It supplies, for example, 90% of the locomotive equipment used in Britain, 50% of the automation equipment and 40% of the electrical machines. It is closely involved in the supply of equipment to publicly-owned and state concerns — for example, it supplies 50% of the turbogenerators installed by the Electricity Boards and 50% of the electronic equipment required by the Ministry of Defence. Obviously then, being in those areas of technology which as the previous chapter explained, require high investment in research and development, it has a large R & D budget — about £70 million a year, in fact — larger than ICI's (£62m) and Shell's (£58m). Hence the title of the article below—'Biggest Science Budget in the Business'.

Philips is an even larger company than GEC. Although GEC has many factories abroad (mostly in Europe and in the Coomonwealth) — in other words, it is an *international* company — most of its activities are conducted in, or directed from, the United Kingdom. Philips on the other hand, as a *multinational* company, has manufacturing plants in 40 countries and its subsidiaries are more independent (and larger) than those of GEC. Philips Gloeilampenfabriken is the overall name of the company, with Philips Electrical and Associated Industries being the British subsidiary. Although Philips, like GEC, is classed in the electrical engineering industry, its products tend to be of a 'lighter' nature than those of GEC. Both are in the domestic appliance, communications and scientific instrument markets, but Philips is not concerned with the manufacture of heavy engineering products, such as turbogenerators. However, the company is involved in various chemical activities (particularly pharmaceuticals) which do not concern GEC. Philips' particular involvement in the radio, television, hi-fi, lighting and educational equipment markets prompts the title of the article on it — 'Lamplight on Electronics for Leisure'.

We suggest you read each article at least twice; the first time, straight through, the second time, reading also the extensive notes and attempting the various questions which follow each article.

Biggest science budget in the business
Nicholas Valery (*New Scientist* Sept 27, 1973)

The £70 million that Sir Arnold Weinstock spends each year on research and development and engineering makes his General Electric Company the biggest industrial R & D organisation in Britain today.

The dishwasher-to-nuclear reactor group has grown out of a series of dramatic mergers and acquisitions executed by Weinstock during the 1960s. Today, the group has a turnover in excess of £1 100 million. Its biggest revenue earners are electronics, telecommunications and automation (£321 million), power engineering (£155 million), components, cables and wires (£132 million), industrial products (£127 million) and consumer wares (£119 million). It has a far better return on capital employed than either of its two European competitors, Siemens and Philips, and a performance that comes close to that of the US giant, General Electric (no relation).[1]

Administering a science budget that, at the last count, was bigger than the UK Atomic Energy Authority's or even the Science Research Council's in a company which employs some 10 000 scientists and engineers and supports them with no fewer than 23 000 technicians, might elsewhere involve endless committees and numerous study groups. At GEC, 90 per cent of the load is delegated to the managing directors of the operating units and their technical directors, with a small monitoring unit at the centre composed of the group's technical director, Robert Clayton, and the research director. Sir Eric Eastwood FRS, radar expert and chief scientist of Marconi prior to its merger with GEC.

Eastwood is no commissar who simply collects a slice of turnover and funnels it through his laboratories. Weinstock's brand of accountancy doesn't work that way. Responsibility for operating costs — not only production and marketing but research and development, too — is handed down to the managers of the individual operating units. And it is their job to decide individually how much to spend out of their own profits on research as well as development. Between them, the divisional managers finance around 60 per cent of the group's research effort — much being spent in GEC's central laboratories. The balance for research comes direct from group profits, plus a fillip in the form of government contracts.

Like a number of other high technology companies, GEC was practising a form of 'customer/contractor' funding of research long before Lord Rothschild proposed the scheme for government science. (Rothschild had himself been the research boss of Shell prior to moving into Cabinet Office.) At GEC, Eastwood and his laboratory directors act as internal contractors, the suppliers of research capacity; while Clayton is its proxy-customer. Says Clayton: 'We have an intelligent customer/

intelligent contractor arrangement here — with me stirring the pot'.[2]

Clayton, who rose from the research ranks of GEC via development and a spell of managing an operating company, is Weinstock's technical eyes and ears — a 'lodger' with access to a staff of 400 people at the group's Hirst Research Centre at Wembley. Back in 1966, Weinstock decided that someone should be appointed to test the group's technological performance and find ways of improving it. Clayton got the job. One of the first things he tried to do was improve the communications between the research laboratories and the operating units. Today, reports are no longer broadcast to all and sundry, but instead are very carefully aimed at those who will be interested. This, claims Clayton, makes report reading no longer a meaningless chore.

Clayton is an experienced research director in his own right, and an articulate thinker on industrial research policy. 'The last thing a company should do,' he says, 'is allocate a fixed percentage of turnover to research . . . First you must ask *Why?* about any piece of new research.' The development of a new product, he adds, should be kept as close as possible to the site of its eventual production and marketing. He agrees emphatically with the sentiment: 'Development, production and marketing is simply one activity.[3]

KEEPING SOME RESEARCH SEPARATE

In a company the size of Weinstock's many of the technological units have some research associated with their development work. 'In fact,' Clayton points out, 'we only distinguish research in GEC as advanced work done at a **separate** site.' Apart from the Hirst Research Centre at Wembley, these 'separate' research sites include the group's Mechanical Engineering Laboratory at Whetstone, associated mainly with GEC Power Engineering, and Marconi's Great Baddow Research Laboratories near Chelmsford. Other research and advanced development facilities in the group include the Trafford Park and Stafford Laboratories of GEC Power Engineering.

But research at GEC is never allowed to become overly precious. Nor does the group deify the 'separateness' of research to anything like the extent as some of its Continental competitors, notably Philips. Nor, still, does it adopt a rigid Rothschild-like surcharge on contractual work, to pay for long-range basic research. A much more flexible approach is used — a strategy being defined by Eastwood and his laboratory directors which is then argued with Clayton as the representative of the rest of the company. This is pursued until modified by fresh ideas and constraints emerging from the scientific community or by changes in the market.

Great store is, in fact, placed on bright research scientists acting as 'gate-keepers'[4]. Ways of keeping them in touch with the outside world include sending them to conferences at home and abroad — not just to listen but to read papers, exchange ideas and participate actively. This willingness and ability to participate and exchange ideas, says GEC, is the basic price of admission to that select club of jet-set technologists who are frequently to be found in and out of each other's laboratories. Clayton tells how, back in 1965, he was singularly impressed by the integrated circuit technology he was shown by semiconductor companies such as Fairchild and Texas Instruments. What he saw convinced him of the need for increased activity, both on integrated circuit developments and on study of applications by GEC equipment makers. One result of the applications study was a forecast in 1966 that TTL (transistor-transistor logic) would become the digital workhorse by the early 1970s. He says: 'This was one of the occasions when we were right!'

Like Philips and Bell Labs, GEC also argues that having some research laboratories separate from the main product divisions provides an excellent 'entry point' in the company for bright young people — who, the management believes, will not all try to make a life-time career in research. 'We've encouraged 50 of our research scientists to move on to development work over the past two years,' boasts Howard Losty, director of the Hirst Research Centre. From there, many will advance their careers further via production, marketing and management. 'Nearly all managers in GEC have science or engineering degrees', says Clayton (himself a visiting professor at Imperial College). 'But you cannot, and must not, generalise. Some individuals will remain brilliant and innovative scientists all their lives . . . We need them, and the necessary supporting staff, to remain in research and make their careers there.'

With their uncommitted central research funds, laboratories such as Hirst, Great Baddow and Whetstone provide an ideal environment for carrying out the early stages — certainly the first few formative years — of projects that have yet to be fully defined. The laboratories also do research which does not have one immediately obvious internal customer — falling between, say, two or more existing production divisions. In these circumstances, central funds are used until a divisional sponsor emerges naturally. Quite often, too, the central research laboratories are the place where new technologies are pioneered and then fed into the company generally (a current example is computer-aided design). And one of the roles of staff in the central laboratories is to provide knowledge of fundamental improvements and know-how in materials and process techniques which operating units will use in the future.

Howard Losty also explains his use of 'no-strings' research funds on the ground that it is usually the cheapest way — often the only way — to get the company's fingers wet in a wholly new area. Clayton adds: 'Our job is to be technically informed and to provide information which will help decisions to be made and things to be done by intention, not by accident.' One example is the work which the company carried out previously in a number of its laboratories on superconductivity. After a period in which substantial effort in this field was not considered to be justified, studies have recently recommenced on superconducting generators, this time in a laboratory associated with an operating unit. This is a long-range study which nevertheless is being carried out by divisional scientists — simply because they happen to be the best people to undertake the work. (Despite this, Clayton admits that he doesn't expect to see a superconducting generator in service with an electricity generating authority in the UK before 1990.)

The separate research centre also provides, of course, a home for all the sophisticated research tools and facilities that would otherwise be too expensive to have scattered and duplicated around the group. Both Bob Clayton and his contractor colleague, Howard Losty, admit that there is some benefit in having the central research laboratories far from the day-to-day pressures of production emergencies. They add, however, that the real strength of laboratories like Hirst is that it fosters a cross-fertilised approach to fresh problems. As such, it is also the ideal location for carrying out thinking about future technologies and, on occasion, future markets. 'In some cases,' Clayton has said, 'it is impossible to forecast likely trends in customer requirements and to couple these with predictions of future technical developments . . . The two forecasts can be brought together in a future-product plan, which can be examined to determine gaps which have to be filled.'[5]

RETURN ON RESEARCH

Clayton admits to having been influenced by a comment once made by Sir James Taylor, formerly of ICI. Once every five years, ICI apparently carried out an exercise to see what profit (or saving) had resulted from its research and development programme. Taylor found, by and large, that the R & D paid for itself — just by making minor improvements to products and processes. The really important advances and discoveries occurred infrequently; indeed, in the development and early commercial exploitation stages these were generally loss-making. Big projects, arising out of fundamental new discoveries or advanced technologies, were found to take years to bring to the profit-making stage — and even then there was no guarantee that they would be major financial successes. These lessons have lodged firmly in Clayton's mind.[6]

That is why, today, discussion figures prominently in planning and running GEC's central research. Particularly important are the involvement of the men actually doing the work and the people in the operating units who may actually use it. Once every six months, for example, researchers write a one or two page note on objectives, achievements and the possible future of their project. On top of this, every Monday morning Howard Losty sits down with three of his working scientists and gives each of them half an hour to explain his project, following this with free discussion and a visit to the laboratory, where the work is being done. Inside the meeting rank is abolished and all are free to comment and criticise. They compare their own work with that of other groups around the world. Sir Eric Eastwood often sits in; Bob Clayton attends meetings that he is particularly interested in. This is research review at grass roots level.

Complete areas of work — such as telecommunications, lamps and lighting, electronic components — are also regularly reviewed with managing directors of operating units and their technical directors, and others in the company who may be deeply concerned. Here Eastwood takes the chair, Losty and his colleagues describe the work being done and planned for the future, and the operating units have the opportunity to comment on their own needs and on the relevance of what is being discussed. Losty also regularly describes the work of the laboratories to Weinstock himself, sending at the same time the relevant extracts from his description to the managing director of each operating unit concerned, so that he may comment or discuss any difference of opinion.

From time to time, Howard Losty and Bob Clayton also set up informal discussions on projects or technical areas (for instance, optical communications or displays) which are attended by both research staff and people from elsewhere in the company; all who are invited are expected to contribute to the discussion and particularly the summing up. 'There is no place here for those who merely wish to sit back and be informed,' says Clayton.

The conventional wisdom about the bigness of big corporations is that they have the resources — human as well as financial — to undertake ventures beyond the scope of lesser firms. Few of the giant industrial groups, however, actually use their prodigious strength to break new technological ground. GEC, in particular, has been more noted for its growth from merger and rationalisation than from increased sales or existing or exciting new products[7]. True, the EE/AEI acquisition five years ago was no mean mouthful; and even a python as powerful as GEC has had its digestion troubles. But now, with an *embarras* of cash (£183 million in 1972–73), the group could once again be ready to digest another electrical/electronics company. Firms such as Plessey, Thorn, BICC and even Hawker Siddeley have each in their turn been suggested as likely morsels. So, too, have some smaller fry like Decca and Racal. (Hawker Siddeley, however, with its strong interests in electrical, mechanical and aircraft engineering and its present excess of liquidity also, presents an interesting possibility of actually being in a position to bid for part of GEC — its 50 per cent holding in British Aircraft Corporation — providing of course, the price were right.)

Like many other large industrial organisations, GEC is fully aware that what it has in terms of resources it might well lack in terms of innovative initiative. 'Small companies can be particularly good at innovation', remarks Clayton, 'but then the resources of big firms are usually needed to carry the innovation through properly . . . Our aim must be to organise ourselves so as to provide the innovative environment of the small company and the benefits of size, without the frustrations that are sometimes encountered in a big company — the last of these grow like weeds, the first two have to be cultivated.'

Weinstock, who to many symbolizes the pinnacle of cost-conscious management, is said by his colleagues to be particularly keen also on innovation. Unfortunately, the City doesn't see it quite like that. Indeed, the stock-market has progressively downrated GEC — down, in fact, from its price-earnings ratio four years ago of more than 25 to a p/e today of around 13, though it has been recovering strongly since publishing its recent accounts. Several financial analysts have actually expressed a lack of confidence about GEC's technological future — suggesting that, while profits should doubtless grow over the next three or four years, the ruthless cash-generation attitude common throughout the group might possibly work against GEC's long-term future.

This, of course, is only an impression. But in the City such gut-feelings can become apparent reality — simply through a general lack of trading interest shown in such shares. The question, then, is: Does GEC today really do enough research and development to ensure that it has the technical competence and new products to remain at the forefront of its field in, say, a decade's time?[8]

The wide spread of GEC's product range — from kitchen ware to advanced technology — makes calculations of R & D as a gross percentage of turnover meaningless. The most one can say is that, given a home sales figure of about £900 million, the proportion spent on research development and advanced engineering is around 8 per cent — thus putting GEC as a group well into the high-technology business (even more so than, say, the Philips group).

The company refuses to release actual breakdowns of R & D expenditure in individual sectors, but estimates based on the size of its various laboratories, and the nature of the work undertaken in them, give some rough guides for evaluation. For instance, about two-thirds of the laboratory effort is clearly devoted to electronics, telecommunications and automation. This suggests that R & D here absorbs about 15 per cent of the combined sales (£321 million) of these sectors. To keep technologically abreast of the competition in power engineering, on the other hand, is much cheaper — generally reckoned to require no more than 6 per cent of sales to be spent on development and engineering (say, £9.3 million in £155 million sales). The remaining £14 million or so of R & D money is probably spread fairly evenly over the other sectors — components, cables and wire, industrial products and consumer wares — giving a mean figure here of about 4 per cent of sales (£378 million).[9]

Such figures, crude though they are, reflect the exceptionally high cost of remaining competitive in the electronics business. While not as deeply committed to semiconductor research as some (a 20 per cent figure is not uncommon), GEC is nevertheless well up with its main competitors here, and can more than hold its own in the other sectors of electrical engineering. Bob Clayton's attitude is that how much a firm commits to research and development depends on the field, the scale and the intentions — in other words, on the company's needs. 'And I've never known Arnold Weinstock cut what an operating manager says he needs,' he says. Last year, in fact, GEC would liked to have spent more on long-range research than it did. 'But', explains Clayton, 'we were limited simply by the number of good people available to spend the money.'

Notes on the GEC article

1. An extensive account of the history of the three principal British Electrical engineering companies — GEC, English Electric, Associated Electrical Industries — and of their mergers of the late nineteen-sixties to produce the current General Electric Company is given in Jones and Marriott (1970). A brief journalistic account can be found in Turner (1971). For a radical analysis of the reasons for the mergers and of the general philosophy of GEC's mode of carrying out its activities see Counter-Information Services (1972).

2. These first three paragraphs set out the main feature of GEC's R & D policy — the customer/contractor' system of funding.

In general, there are *two* ways in which any R & D activity can be funded. Firstly, the particular organisation carrying out the research (be it a company's R & D department, a university department, a government research unit or a private research establishment) can simply be given a certain sum of money by some funding body (a company board of directors, a government committee, a public foundation or a private individual). The money will usually be given with a proviso that it should be used to investigate problems in a specific area of work; but this area can be very broadly defined and the selection of the actual research projects to be carried out, and the general direction of the research itself, will be left entirely in the hands of those doing the work — namely the management of the research laboratory, workshop or unit.

The second method of funding R & D — called the 'customer/contractor' system — applied the idea of 'he who pays the piper, calls the tune'. Instead of just giving a sum of money for the research organisation to spend almost as it wishes, the supplier of the funds (the 'customer') states much more specifically what development it wants doing or what problem it wants investigating and invites research organisations to perform this work for a relatively fixed sum — in other words, research is put out to contract. It is this principle that Lord Rothschild (who, until mid-1974 was head of the Government's 'think-tank') proposed should govern the distribution of funds overseen by the various Research Councils which are responsible for the funding of much research in medical, agricultural and environmental research institutes in the UK. As the article points out, GEC does not organise the funding of its R & D by the first method — the head of research at GEC, Sir Eric Eastwood, does not 'collect a slice of the turnover' from the company and decide himself what research and development projects his research laboratories will do. Instead, the management of the various divisions of GEC decide what R & D they want to do and they request GEC's research department to do the necessary work for a certain sum which the divisions themselves provide out of their own funds.

Now there are a number of problems here relating to the general questions raised above. If all GEC's R & D were to be funded on the 'customer/contractor' system, then are there not dangers to the long-term technological and scientific progress of the company? The costs incurred in the discovery of new scientific ideas or the invention and development of new products are not something that can be exactly predicted in advance. Obviously then, the management of GEC's divisions (who are expected by the managing director to ensure that they make adequate, or hopefully, continually increasing, profits) will be wary of proposing research projects whose success they cannot be sure of and whose costs are totally unpredictable. So does not the 'customer/contractor' system, despite its advantages in keeping research departments alive to the requirements of the company they work for, discourage the discovery and development of new ideas and products to the detriment of the longer term development (or even survival) of the company?

How do you think this could be avoided while preserving the necessary close relationship between the 'needs' of the company, as perceived by the divisional managers, and the nature of the research being carried out?

3. As was explained in the last chapter, a firm's investment in R & D can be seen as one way by which it attempts to increase (or maintain at an acceptable level) its profits. But saying that does not get us very far when we are considering a particular firm's detailed activities. In principle, there is a multitude of research projects on which the company's research budget could be spent. Therefore there must be many projects which are rejected for lack of available funds which managers of research activities suspect could, possibly, be more profitable than those projects which are actually carried out. The problem therefore of deciding what the overall R & D budget should be so as, on the one hand, not to waste resources but, on the other hand, not to miss a possibly highly profitable opportunity is one which individual companies have considerable difficulty with.

Often the percentage of turnover allocated to research, that Clayton mentions, could be established by comparison with other firm's R & D expenditures in the same industry — a firm would try and be as 'research intensive' as the industry in general. Such 'rule of thumb' methods are only of use in the short run; in the long run a firm would need to adjust its research intensity by taking into account actual calculations of expected profitability of particular research and development projects modified by knowledge of the profitability of alternative uses of funds. The economist, Edwin

Mansfield (1968) has studied this question in American industry and he concludes that indeed firms do modify their R & D expenditures to take these factors into account.

Clayton, following GEC's policy of strict questioning of all expenditure rejects the 'rule-of-thumb' approach to the setting of R & D expenditures. He goes further than this, however, in emphasising that research is not an activity on its own. The purpose of new product research in a firm is to come up with new ideas which, after suitable development, can be put into production and sold at a sufficient profit leading to the survival (or expansion) of the firm. But all these activities have to be closely integrated — they have to be seen as 'simply one activity'. The popular idea of how scientists and technologists ply their trade — namely that they 'discover' things and come up with new ideas, completely isolated from what the organisation they work for wants (or is able) to produce and sell *profitably* — is rejected by Clayton. In this view the purpose of the firm is to sell things; therefore all the firm's activities, including those involved in R & D, should be directed towards this end.

There is plenty of evidence to support the view that most of those 'new ideas' (innovations) which are successful, from the individual firm's point of view, were assisted in their success by the firm's concern that research, development, production and marketing should be closely integrated — that, to put it crudely, research should be organised to satisfy the consumer's requirements, as perceived by the firm's marketing organisations. One particular important study of successful innovations was done in Sussex University — the SAPPHO study. They reported their study and results as follows:

THE PROJECT

Project SAPPHO is a study of the innovation process in two science-based sectors of industry. It was conceived as a systematic attempt to identify and evaluate the factors which distinguish innovations which have achieved commercial success from those which have not. Existing studies deal almost exclusively with innovations that were commercially successful, although observation shows that in reality attempts at innovation are frequently unsuccessful. It was therefore thought worthwhile to attempt a study of failed innovations alongside parallel successes. There is an abundance of literature on the subject of innovation, largely hypothesising about the conditions under which it flourishes. The hypotheses put forward cover almost every conceivable aspect of the innovation process, and some of them conflict. Typically, studies of innovation have highlighted 'single factors' in the process, of which the ultimate success is believed to have hinged. Accepting that innovation is a complex sequence of events, involving scientific research as well as technological development, management, production and selling, it was felt that these single factor interpretations were less than satisfactory, and that allowances should be made for multi-factor explanations. Furthermore, it was considered that insufficient attention had been given to inter-industry differences and that in consequence generalisations had been made that might not apply to all sectors of industry.

Project SAPPHO drew its examples from two industries, chemicals and scientific instruments, and applied the technique of pairing attempts at innovation. The team completed and analysed 29 such pairs, 17 in chemicals and 12 in instruments. Each pair consisted of one commercially successful and one less successful attempt to innovate, both attempts being aimed at the same market. The history of every innovation was recorded, mainly by interview in depth of the individuals involved, although background material was provided by searching the technical and scientific literature relevant to the innovation. A documented version of each attempt, agreed by the individuals concerned, and covering all aspects of the process from the initial research and development through to marketing, was used to provide information for a large number of measures comparing the characteristics of the successful innovation with those of its less successful counterpart. The results of the project were derived from statistical analysis of the 29 sets of information so obtained, and include both an examination of the underlying structure of the data and the testing of various existing hypotheses. It should be noted that nearly 60 potential pairs were identified and investigated to achieve a set of 29.

THE RESULTS

The results show clearly that the attempt to search for explanations involving more than one facet of the innovation process is justified. The differences observed between the successful and unsuccessful innovations cannot be explained by superiority in any one aspect of the process. To this extent SAPPHO differs from the majority of previous studies. The clear-cut differences within pairs which do fall into a consistent pattern distinguishing between success and failure can be summarised in five statements:

1. Successful innovators were seen to have a much better understanding of user needs. They may acquire this superiority in a variety of different ways. Some may collaborate intimately with potential customers to acquire the necessary knowledge of user requirements. Others may use thorough market studies. However acquired, this imaginative understanding is one of the

hallmarks of success. Conversely failures often ignore users' requirements or even disregard their views.

2. Successful innovators pay much more attention to marketing. Failures were sometimes characterised by neglect of market research, publicity and user education, and the failure to anticipate customer problems.

3. Successful innovators perform their development work more efficiently than failures, but not necessarily more quickly. They eliminate technical defects from the product or process **before** they launch it. They usually employ a larger development team on the project, and spend more money on it. This applies even where the successful firm is smaller.

4. Successful innovators make more effective use of outside technology and scientific advice, even though they perform more of the work in-house. They have better contacts with the scientific community not in general but in the *specific* area concerned.

5. The responsible individuals in the successful attempts are usually more senior and have greater authority than their counterparts who fail. In the instrument industry they have more diverse experience, often including experience abroad. The greater power of the individual innovators in the successful attempts facilitates the concentration of effort on the scale which is needed as well as the integration of R & D and marketing.

The results of testing existing hypotheses on the SAPPHO data must be considered in the light of the main finding, that no single factor can by itself explain the success-failure difference. However, some of the previously advanced single factor explanations are supported by inclusion in the group of capabilities that appear to differentiate successful attempts from unsuccessful ones. These include those hypotheses which relate success to market awareness and marketing effort, those which emphasise the importance of individuals, particularly with managerial responsibility, and those hypotheses which relate success to R & D capability and efficiency, and which have stressed the importance of effective communications, both internal and external, in innovating firms. The results do not support the belief that size of firm is a determining factor, that successful innovation results either from strong or weak market positions, that greater familiarity with the technology or the market is a necessary ingredient, or that successful innovators take larger (or smaller) risks than unsuccessful ones. It is encouraging to find that there is broad agreement between these results and those of two earlier studies in other industries, those of Carter and Williams (1957) and Marquis and Myers (1970).

The results should not be looked upon as a recipe to ensure automatic success for innovators who apply it. Indeed many of the factors which distinguish success from failure are not of a kind which are easily created within a firm, at least in the short run. An analogy with football may help to clarify the situation. Both in football and in competitive industrial innovation there will always be winners and losers. This is the nature of the game*. Knowledge of those factors which are conducive to success may lead some firms and some football teams to succeed more often than others by applying this kind of knowledge. But theor competitors will also learn, so that circumstances are constantly changing and the end-result may simply be an improvement in the standard of 'play' all round. The managers of football teams mostly know what their teams ought to do in order to win, but the factors which they are striving to control are not easy to manipulate and they certainly cannot guarantee success in any particular game. What can be much more positively asserted is that a team which has not learnt to adapt its tactics and level of fitness to contemporary standards will find itself dropping to the bottom of the League table. To learn the 'rules' of innovation management may sometimes lead to well-earned success, depending upon the relative efforts of competitors and an element of chance. Not to know the 'rules' or to apply them is likely to have the opposite effect. However, even where no competition is involved, technical and market uncertainties are such that failures will continue to occur.

From Science Policy Research Unit (1972). See also Freeman (1974) Chapter 5.

4. The notion of the gatekeeper emerges from work done by T.J. Allen in the USA. It was known that technologists spent very little time reading the technical literature. Allen was able to show that they kept abreast of developments outside the organisation through 'gatekeepers' — individuals who had all the contacts with the appropriate scientific or technical community and/or kept abreast of the literature. These 'gatekeepers' passed information into the organization by means of informal discussions with their colleagues. For more details see Allen (1970).

*Circumstance might conceivably be different in a socialist non-competitive economy insulated from the world market.

5. As was pointed out in note 2, GEC is very concerned that the research and development it carries out should be closely tied up with the requirements of specific divisions of the company. We raised the question of the clash that could result between the inevitably short-term requirements of these divisions and the longer-term requirements of consumers and of the firm's employees and shareholders to ensure that the firm keeps sufficiently abreast of potential technological developments to enable it to keep business and thus provide new products, employment and dividends, well into the future. In these three paragraphs, we see that GEC claims to be doing this longer-term research into technology for the future, though as we shall describe below not everyone accepts these claims.

6. We have already described why firms do R & D at all. This paragraph in the article emphasises the points we have made. Most research in industry does not involve amazing discoveries or astounding inventions. In fact the problems of turning a potentially important invention, important in its impact on the firm and on society, into a product that can be sold at a *profit* are so enormous because the impact is so uncertain — that most firms do not go looking for such inventions. They concentrate on small 'improvements' in the products themselves or in the techniques involved in manufacturing them.

7. Despite what seem to be enormous sums spent on R & D by industry this spending represents only a small part of the total cost of introducing new products on to the market. It has been estimated that 'research' accounts on average for 5–10% of the total cost of launching a new product and 'development' accounts for another 10–20%; the remaining 70–85% goes on the reorganisation of production, new investments and marketing. Thus for any significant new technology to have any chance of being successfully introduced to consumers it must be introduced by firms sufficiently large enough, in terms of financial and organisational resources, to be able to afford the very high costs. It would seem reasonable to assume then that the majority of research and development effort would be found in the largest firms. This is, in fact the case. Those American manufacturing firms which, in 1961, had over 5000 employees, accounting for 41% of all employment and 47% of all sales, accounted for 86% of all research and development. Norris and Vaizey (1973) have summarised the main points concerning the relationship between R & D expenditure and firm size (p.63/64)

> The first point is that there is some minimum size of firm below which it is not worth undertaking any research and

development — at least that can be identified as such. This, by its nature, is not a conclusion that shows up in the sort of statistics that we have considered. There seems little doubt, however, that it is so. The reasoning is as follows. A scientist, with support facilities, costs something around £10 000 in the UK in 1971. It is generally thought unlikely that a firm will devote more than 1.5% of its costs to research and development, so that annual costs of £1½ million represent some such absolute minimum. That is not to say that firms of less than a certain size will spend nothing, for firms are so arbitrary in their definition of what constitutes research and development that some expenditure may appear almost anywhere in the statistics. Some activities of production engineers, for example, may be classed as 'development' when they are not, and some development work may appear as 'overheads'.[*]

Secondly, large firms undertake the major part of all industrial research and development. In the USA, the 300 largest companies account for 92% of research expenditure and the 40 largest companies account for 70%. A similar concentration is thought to hold in the UK. Therefore, any analysis of industrial research must concentrate on the activities of large firms.

Thirdly, the larger the company, the more likely it is that it will have **some** research activities. In the USA virtually all firms with over 5000 employees undertake some research, while only one in ten of companies with under 500 employees do so.

Fourthly, of all the companies who do spend money on research, it does not seem in general to be true that large firms are more research intensive than medium sized firms are.

Fifthly, although the great bulk of research and development takes place in large firms, significant inventions have emanated from small firms and from individuals. A classic case is xerography. The process was patented, in 1940, by an individual, Carlson, who subsequently approached a number of companies to see if they were interested in developing it. All the major office equipment companies turned him down, but eventually a small photographic company, Haloid, took up the invention. Subsequently, the corporation experienced very rapid growth and, by 1968, Xerox Corporation, as it is now named, ranked 109th in the Fortune list. Many other examples could be cited, (Jewkes, Sawers and Shillerman, 1969).

[*]It has constantly to be borne in mind that research and development covers a multitude of activities. An anecdote may serve to illustrate this. A manager was discussing how activities are allocated to research and development: 'If Jack is asked to repair a machine and he succeeds, it's maintenance. If he fails, it's research.'

Norris and Vaizey's fourth point alludes to the fact that, in some industries, although the bulk of R & D is done by the larger firms, medium-sized firms often spend more on R & D in *proportion to their size.* This is particularly so in the American pharmaceutical and scientific instrument industries where the largest firms (over 10 000 employees) have research intensities of 5.1% and 6.4% respectively, whereas for the medium size-firms (5 000—9 999 employees) the research intensities are 8.6% and 8.1% respectively. Freeman (1974), Chapter 6, discusses the relationship at length.

8. This paragraph asks specifically the question we have continuously raised in the notes to this article. Investors, by their 'general lack of trading interest' in GEC's shares, and financial analysts seem to have some doubts about the company's longer-term future. And they are not alone in this. Two weeks after the publication of this article in *New Scientist* a letter appeared in the same magazine from a officer of the trade union called the Association of Scientific, Technical and Managerial Staffs (ASTMS). We reproduce this letter here.

GEC's SCIENCE BUDGET

Sir, — It was with total disbelief that I read the article, 'Biggest science budget in the business,' on the enormous efforts being made by the General Electric Company in research and development. We as an association represent some 30 000 GEC technical, supervisory and management employees and are perhaps in a position of being slightly better briefed than your magazine.

The amount of cash spent by the Weinstock organisation on pure research and development is miniscule. It was clear at the time that GEC took over AEI and subsequently merged with the English Electric organisation that research and development that was not directly product-exploitable would be so severely pruned as to make its future contribution irrelevant within the industry.

We have seen research establishments in the last four years whose employees were making useful contributions, but with perhaps little profit motivation, either closed or so restricted in budget as to make them unviable.

Yes, the company does employ 10 000 scientists and engineers, and yes it does employ 23 000 technicians in support, but these are not used, apart from a few hundred at North Wembley, on anything which could remotely be regarded as research, although no doubt the company would argue that they are used on development, development which we would say was the exploitation of current product generation, and will provide no foundation for the future of the electrical engineering industry in this country.

We have talked to the company at all levels, we have raised the question with our members in the House of Commons. Neither they nor the company could provide us with any assurance that there was a future for the scientist or the academic engineer within the General Electric Company.

We would criticise each and every paragraph of your lengthy report. Clearly the source for the article was gleaned from the company and not from those employees or organisations that do not need to justify the exploitation of this new technology industry for profit.

We will not quarrel with Weinstock's ability to produce from five merged companies an exceedingly fine balance sheet, nor will we misunderstand the reasons why he is in business, but no employee of the General Electric Company could be a party to misleading the public into thinking that there is an enormous budget commitment into science and the future of the industry by the General Electric Company.

D. Groves
Association of Scientific, Technical and Managerial Staffs
Birmingham B15 1PJ
From *New Scientist* 18th October 1973, p. 215

It is clear from this letter that the ASTMS does not consider that GEC does enough of the *right kind* of research to ensure the firm's survival (and therefore its employee's jobs) in the decade to come. GEC does employ 33 000 scientific workers but, according to the ASTMS, they are 'not used . . . . on anything which could remotely be regarded as research', although it is admitted that 'a few at North Wembley' are so employed, at GEC's research centre where GEC concentrates its longer-term speculative work. ASTMS claims that most of GEC's scientific workers are employed on *development work* and that such work is only concerned with 'exploitation of current product generation' (ie. small changes in existing products) and will not provide the British electrical engineering industry with an adequate 'foundation for the future'. Thus GEC cannot assure ASTMS that there will be a future 'for the scientist or the academic engineer' in the company.

Such criticisms highlight the problem we have been focussing on — namely, the possible contradiction that exists between the 'need' for a firm to harness its R & D effort to increasing its short-term gains and the 'need' for it to have sufficient technological knowledge to ensure that it will still be in business in ten or more years time.

This possible contradiction is not of course confined to GEC's R & D policy. A survey was carried out in the USA in 1961 to establish how soon different industries expected results from their R & D programmes — that is, what their 'pay-back' periods were. A sample of the answers is shown in *Table 9*, adapted from Mansfield (1968), p. 15.

Table 9   Expected average pay-back periods from R & D expenditures, 1961 (US industry)

Industry	% of companies answering survey Pay out period		
	3 yrs.	4–5 yrs.	6+ yrs.
Iron and steel	38	50	12
Automobiles & trucks	54	40	6
Chemicals	33	41	26
Rubber	38	38	24
Textiles	76	24	0
Petroleum & coal products	17	33	50
Electrical machinery	61	32	7
All manufacturing	55	34	11

The chemical type industries appeared to have longer pay-back periods whereas three-quarters of the textile firms had a very short period. As you can see nine-tenths of all manufacturing companies expected their research and development work to pay back in less than six years and 55% expected a pay back in three years. In other words half of American manufacturing companies in 1961 expected to have profitable results from their R & D programmes before 1965.

9. In this paragraph Valery has calculated the spending on R & D for various divisions of GEC, expressed as a percentage of the total sales (turnover) of the divisions — 15% for electronics, telecommunications and automation, 6% for power engineering and 4% for industrial and consumer products. These figures are *not* the *research intensities* for the various divisions. Research intensities, as the last chapter discussed, are stated by expressing R & D expenditure as a percentage of the *net output* of the industry concerned. Nevertheless figures relating R & D expenditure to turnover on an industry basis are available — for the electronics industry the figure is 12.1%, for electrical machinery 3.2% and for electrical engineering overall 6.1%. Comparing these industry figures with those for GEC shows, as Valery is trying to demonstrate, that GEC spends more than many of its competitors on R & D.

Lamplight on electronics for leisure
Nicholas Valery (*New Scientist*, April 5, 1973)

Founded 80 years ago on the strength of an idea for making
cheap filaments for electric light bulbs, Philips has become one
of the most successful of Europe's home-grown multinational
corporations. With manufacturing plants in 40 countries and
sales organisations in 60, the company today employs more than
370 000 people worldwide — and reputedly makes nearly a
million different products. As this article shows, Philips takes
special care to separate development from research — to ensure
that the former is real product development, and the latter
sufficiently free from commercial restraints to be able to plan
the company's products for a decade hence.

An apocryphal story is told at Philips, the giant Dutch
electrical group, about a mythical research director of a large
stationery supplier who unveiled before sceptical board members
a machine he had developed comprising a roller and 40 keys.
'This, gentlemen,' he said, 'is the future of the pencil and
paper.' Within minutes the new invention — which they had
quickly dubbed a 'typewriter' — was dismissed as impractical.
Was it not, after all, 500 times more expensive, 1 000 times
heavier and five times slower than their existing product? Moreover, the pencil was very nearly 100 per cent reliable and
required only do-it-yourself maintenance. The downcast
inventor picked up his machine and went home.

Today, Philips is reckoned to spend close on £40 million
annually on research and development — and has good cause
to remember the typewriter story. Back in 1935, company
executives predicted that the initial price of television —
estimated at around £120 per set — would never fall to within
the reach of the mass market. Their scientists were equally
pessimistic, adding that, for convincing technical reasons,
television would catch on only in areas of very high population
density.[1]

The lesson has taught Philips to look at the future with
particular care, and to be ready always for the unexpected. To
this end, the company today ploughs nearly 1.5 per cent of its
world-wide sales (£2750 million in 1972) back into its six
research laboratories — at Eindhoven, Redhill, Hamburg,
Aachen, Paris and Brussels — and into its product development
offices. Between them, the research laboratories employ no less
than 4000 people, one out of four of whom are 'graduate
equivalents' (continental PhDs). Just over half the research staff
— 2300 people — are located in the main laboratories in south-
east Holland. Second in size are the Mullard Research

Laboratories at Redhill in Surrey, which employ some 600 people, including about 190 graduate-equivalents. It is the job of these laboratories, guided by a top level research council that is answerable to only the main board, to ensure that the company as a whole has a well-filled technological store house ready to meet the challenges of the future.

NV Philips Gloeilampenfabrieken was founded in 1891 by a Dutchman, Gerard Philips, who had developed a cheap way of making incandescent light bulbs. The first lamp filaments were made of cellulose. But when tungsten became available in 1903, the fledgling company quickly found a need for some rudimentary materials research. A decade later, with Philips the biggest light bulb maker in Europe, the company hired itself a research director, Dr. Gilles Holst. Renowned for his work on super-conductivity in Kamerlingh Onnes' pioneering cryogenics laboratory at Leyden University, Holst established a vigorous research group which soon acquired a reputation for making important contributions in material research and electrical phenomena. It was Holst, too, who laid the foundations of the research philosophy that continues to this day.

To Holst, understanding the incandescent lamp led naturally to research on thermionic tubes, and the end of the First World War saw Philips diversifying into radio. By the late 1930s, the firm had carved a 20 per cent slice out of the world market for radio receivers. By then television, despite the company's initial hesitation, was just around the corner — at least, in research terms.

Today, Philips is firmly in the leisure business, with its main product lines — radio, television, and record players — contributing nearly 20 per cent of overall sales. Lighting equipment accounts for only 12 per cent of turnover. The other main product lines are electronic components (12 per cent), domestic appliances (8 per cent), telecommunications and defense equipment (8 per cent), and electro-acoustic products such as tape recorders and broadcasting equipment (6 per cent). The balance comes from assorted sales of industrial, medical and environmental equipment, computers and, of course, phonograph records.

After an agonising decade of deteriorating profits, Philips has now begun to reap the benefits of being a multi-national firm in an expanding market. While turnover quintupled between 1959 and 1971, earnings remained roughly constant in guilder equivalent terms. Last year, however, profits were up 70 per cent to around £80 million; and this year profits have risen to £99 million, indicating that one of the most extensive reorganisations ever undertaken in a large European corporation is now complete.

Ever since Holst's early days, Philips has maintained an enlightened view about research; it is the only way, the firms says, of buying options on the future. Out of the Eindhoven laboratories, for instance, came the pentode tube, invented by B.D.H. Tellegen. By incorporating a third (suppressor) grid into the thermionic vacuum tube, this made really high amplification of radio signals possible for the first time. From the same laboratory also came the Penning gauge, still used extensively in vacuum equipment and the basis of the modern ionic pumps used for achieving ultra-high vacuum conditions. Another important contribution from Eindhoven was J.L. Snoek's development of ferrites as low loss magnetic materials for use at high frequencies in electronic devices. The same laboratory also produced Ferroxdure, the first non-metallic permanent magnet to be discovered since lodestone.

More recently, Philip's scientists have been in the news for making basic improvements to the Stirling cycle, the basis both of cryogenic equipment for liquifying gases and an engine that can run on a variety of fuels, producing particularly clean exhaust gases. Another well-publicised recent development from Eindhoven is the LOCOS process for fabricating integrated circuits.

Innovations such as these generate a great number of patents. Between them, the six research laboratories and the development offices attached to the company's individual product divisions have created a vast patent portfolio — some 72 000 actual rights and applications stemming from 11 000 different inventions. Over the years it has become company policy to grant licenses to outside firms wishing to manufacture products based on Philips' know-how. The 'Compact Cassette' adopted almost universally for portable tape recorders is one of the company's more successful examples.[2]

CORNERSTONE OF RESEARCH POLICY

Ten commandments of good research management, formulated originally by Gilles Holst, have been collected together by Professor Hendrik Casimir. One, in particular, forms the cornerstone of Philips' present laboratory policy — 'never allow the product divisions any budgetary control over the laboratory's choice of research projects'. Professor Casimir, who succeeded Holst in 1946 and retired from Philips last year, recalls how his predecessor always insisted on a 'considerable degree of independence for the research laboratories . . . they reported to the top management of the company, not to the division.' Casimir also inherited a tradition that was strongly against detailed budgeting. One important result was that the cost of the research work that led to a specific product was never included in the initial launch costs of that product.[3]

This principle manifests itself today in the form of a levy on sales that is imposed on all divisions, the lump sum then being allocated to the six research laboratories according to a plan agreed by a council comprising research directors and various members of the board. Thus none of the research funds are labelled according to source. 'All divisions are entitled to assistance from research laboratories,' says Casimir, 'but not on a pro rata basis . . . In this way we can have long established divisions like the lamp works supporting, say, solid state physics.'

Of course, should the research laboratories ever fail to deliver the goods to the product development groups in the divisions, they would quickly lose their privileged position in the company. But because the divisions themselves have to pay for the research without having a say in its planning, they are naturally keen to participate in new projects (to obtain value for money) and to have their own projects taken up by the central laboratories (to reduce their own overheads). For their part, the research directors frankly admit that they tend to be better at inventing components rather than devising new systems; the latter, they say, are best handled by seconding laboratory staff to the divisions to work alongside the resident engineers.

Some members of the research staff at Eindhoven joke that there is a right way, a wrong way, and a Philips' way of managing research. The corporate structure adopted is, however, the result of a great deal of experience — and clearly a useful model for a number of other well diversified companies that depend on a significant research and development effort. Unlike such specialised giants as ITT, which supports its almost exclusively telephone business with one enormous research and development facility (Bell Labs), the more diverse Philips aims at bringing product development and manufacturing as close together as possible, while keeping research and advanced development sufficiently remote from the commercial environment to save it from being inhibited by day to day pressures from product managers wanting new ideas for immediate sale. The central research laboratories in Eindhoven — perhaps more than Philips' other research centres in Britain, Germany, Belgium and France — play a particularly strategic role in the company's affairs.[4]

From his 26 years' experience at Eindhoven, Casimir makes three particular points worth remembering. First, not all basic results lead to industrial applications. Secondly, the scientific importance of the basic results does not always go hand in glove with their usefulness. Finally, doing basic research provides a sound training for tackling practical problems in a scientific way.[5] Certainly, there are numerous research scientists in Philips who have later had successful careers in technical and even commercial posts in production divisions. Indeed, such a transfer is encouraged by the laboratories — largely to keep down the median age (36 years) of their scientific and technical staff.

Philips remains essentially an electronics-based company, despite its (none too spectacular) foray into medical, chemical, and pharmaceutical products. And today innovations in electronics are becoming increasingly difficult to pursue — not so much because of any failure of research and development but because of the precipitous nature of their economics. Professor G.W. Rathenau, the new director of the Eindhoven laboratories, points to the high risk involved in developing small series of very advanced electronic components. 'It requires a great deal of entrepreneurial courage to invest perhaps $100 million in the mass production of a new device,' says Rathenau. 'This is particularly dangerous when interest rates are not far below 10 per cent.' Occasionally defense contracts help to remove the risk element — but military research expenditure in the Netherlands is insignificant compared with the Pentagon's or even the UK Defense Ministry's.[6]

A glimpse of the future can be seen today in Rathenau's laboratories, where the research spearhead is taking Philips ever deeper into electronic systems for communication, education and entertainment. And it is here that two serious disequilibria have been identified, both arising out of previous erratic developments in information technology. The two points are neatly put by Dr. K. Teer, head of the Laboratory's electronic systems division. 'There is too much telecommunication and too little information; there is too much information and too little communication.'

'It is not enough simply to pile data upon data and opinion upon expectation,' says Teer. 'There is a great and pressing need to dam the stream of information and to hand over the initiative to the individual.' In this context, Teer finds the newspaper a more agreeable medium than television, a phonograph record better than radio, the video cassette better than cable television, and cable television slightly better than broadcast television. Likewise, retrieval facilities at data centres are more attractive

61

than archives. 'It is not the sending of information that has primarily to be speeded up,' says Teer, 'but the process of looking up the information — the process of retrieval.'

ELECTRONICS FOR 1984

With the forecasters reckoning on world sales of electronic communications media rising from today's $9 billion (billion = 10^9) to $38 billion in 1984, the research projects underway behind the closed doors at Eindhoven are no doubt aimed at cashing in on this boom early next decade. The research staff are non-committal about progress, but Teer declares he expects to see three-dimensional colour television sets in American homes by 1980, two-way cable television by 1985, and a facsimile news service in the home by 1990. 'I am convinced,' says Teer, 'that in 1984 the video cassette recorder and the video disc will have found a place, and will undergo the same flourishing development as colour TV today.'[7]

With the 'technological rate of exchange' between Britain and the Netherlands now about double the standard rate of 7.25 guilders to the pound sterling, clear advantages exist for Philips to transfer an increasing number of future research projects from Eindhoven to its Mullard Research Laboratories at Redhill in Surrey. 'There are signs that this is already beginning to happen,' admits Mullard's director, Professor Kurt Hoselitz.[8]

Apart from being the second largest research laboratory in the group, Mullard is unique in having a project application scheme designed to encourage staff members at all levels to submit their own research proposals. Application is made merely by completing a 20-question check list and giving gut-feelings about feasibility, cost, and market potential. Half of the 260 projects proposed since the scheme began in 1969 have already been completed. 'Their success rate is fantastically high,' claims Hoselitz.

Wherever Philips chooses to do its research in the future, there is no doubt that extra care will always be given to providing a highly creative environment. It was Professor Casimir who once said: 'We try to remember that organisation is a necessary evil, not a goal in itself, and that our first duty is to make it possible for really original scientists to work in our laboratories.'

Notes on the Philips article

1. The story in the first paragraph, about a 'large stationery supplier'

missing the chance to be the first to introduce the typewriter on to the market, is an amusing one. Obviously, an invention which would result in a product so much more expensive, heavy, slow and un-reliable than the current product would hardly be likely to appeal to the company. One wonders how many inventions with the type-writer's potential are lying around *at the moment* because their inventors have not been able to convince present-day companies that the invention is a viable proposition, both technically and economically! This leads us to ask two questions concerning the introduction of new products into the market and into society.

Firstly, how can those responsible for transforming technical ideas into profitable and acceptable products decide which ideas have potential and which do not? Secondly, suppose the product the firm is introducing is a 'better' (ie. cheaper or safer or resource-saving), technique of making something, how does this technique spread throughout the relevant industry, transforming an individual firm's advantage into a generalised social 'gain'?

The second question has been studied in some depth by economists in the concept of the 'diffusion of innovations'. See Norris and Vaizey (1973), or Mansfield (1968), or Nabseth and Ray (1974).

As to the first question — how can firms assess the benefits which will accrue to them and/or to society? — the simplest answer is, they find it very difficult. The largest proportion of a firm's R & D expenditure is devoted to limited product and process improvements, so it is not too difficult to calculate their economic benefits to the firm, given that the vast majority of firms expect their R & D expenditure to pay back within five years. However, forecasting the benefits of more substantial technical developments is usually much more difficult. The benefits from large cost or quality improvements in the production of basic materials or components may be easier to forecast since such products are almost certain to be in demand in ten ot twenty years time; but benefits from new consumer articles are almost unpredictable, for who can know what tastes will be in one or two decades?

2. Patents. You can read more about the economic function of patents in Norris and Vaizey (1973) p. 42—47. They analyse the 'dilemma which arises from inventive activity', the contradiction which is apparent between the right of the owners of invention (protected by law through the patent) to use it as they think fit (which includes the right *not* to use it or not to let anyone else use it) and the needs of society in general to get the full advantage of the invention in terms of a better use of resources or a new product, the benefits from which accrue to society as a whole rather than merely to the

inventor. In Norris and Vaizey's view the present system of granting patents 'strikes some sort of compromise between the case for making information about inventions widely available at a low cost, and the case for rewarding the inventor with monopoly profit'.

You might like to sketch out how they come to this conclusion.

3. Dr. Casimir's 'Ten Commandments' governing the directing of research are as follows. In particular, look at No. 8.

1. Engage competent scientists, if possible young, but with academic research experience.

2. Do not pay too much attention to details of their previous experience.

3. Give them a good deal of freedom and accept their idiosyncrasies.

4. Let them publish and participate in international scientific meetings.

5. Steer a middle course between individualism and strict regimentation; base authority on real competence; in case of doubt, favour anarchy.

6. Do not divide a laboratory according to different disciplines, but create mutlidisciplinary teams.

7. Give the research laboratories independence in choice of subjects, but see to it that leaders and staff are thoroughly aware of their responsibility for the future of the whole company.

8. Do not try to run the research laboratories on a detailed budget system and never allow product divisions to have budgetary control over research projects.

9. Encourage the transfer of competent senior people from research laboratories to development laboratories of product divisions.

10. In choosing research projects be guided not only by market possibilities, but also by the state of science.

What would GEC's research director think of this? (see notes 2 and 3 to the article on GEC).

In fact, what would GEC's research director think of the 'Ten Commandments' as a whole? Explain why he would differ.

Draft out a similar list for GEC, based on your knowledge of GEC's research system.

4. Valery gives the three models as follows

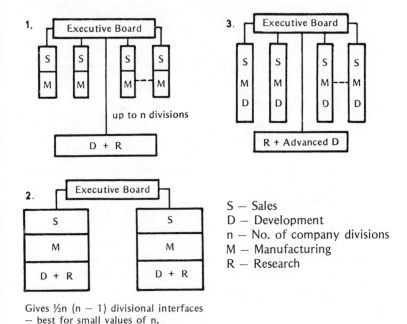

1.

up to n divisions

3.

2.

Gives ½n (n − 1) divisional interfaces
− best for small values of n.

S − Sales
D − Development
n − No. of company divisions
M − Manufacturing
R − Research

According to Valery Model 1 is ITT and Model 3 is Philips. Which one is GEC?

5. 'Basic research' can be defined as research which is undertaken with no specific commercial objectives. Casimir's opinion that basic research should be carried on in industrial research organisations (which presumably should be doing work with commercial objectives in mind) because[1] it provides a sound training for tackling practical problems in a scientific way' is one justification for spending any money on basic research in Philips. Philips are certainly not alone in their view. *Table 10* gives details of the distribution of R & D spending into the various 'categories' of R & D for British industry.

For Manufacturing industry as a whole, 4% was spent on basic research, 21.7% on applied research and 74.3% on development. The 4% represents a total of £25 million. So, although basic research accounts for only a small proportion of R & D expenditure, firms must see (or think they see) some benefit from basic research. Casimir's reason is not the only benefit. Although basic research is very uncertain, with pay off periods much longer than most firms insist on for other research, in some industries it seems to have sufficient potential to

Table 10 Distribution of funds for performance of different types of R & D in UK — all industry 1969—70. Data from Central Statistical Office (1973)

	% of that industry's R & D funds devoted to:		
	Basic research	Applied research	Development
Iron and steel	7.3	53.0	39.7
Motor vehicles	1.2	11.4	87.4
Chemical & petroleum prods.	7.9	43.2	48.9
Rubber	0.5	41.5	58.0
Textiles and man-made fibres	3.3	38.6	58.1
Electrical machinery	3.3	38.0	58.7
Aerospace	2.0	9.0	89.0
Scientific instruments	4.7	17.8	77.6

justify expenditure considerably above average. This is particularly so in the chemical industry. Whether this is because basic research in the chemical industries does provide sufficient new ideas (rather than just background knowledge) or because research is organised by those who *think* it does is a difficult question to answer. As Norris and Vaizey put it, 'Firms generally seek to be profit-maximising, but often they do not know how best to maximise profits and erroneously attach too great a weight to the likely profitable results of a basic research breakthrough'. (Norris and Vaizey (1973) summarise why firms do not do much basic research on p. 56—59 of their book.)

So although some see virtue in doing basic research, in general firms are content to let it be done by other establishments — in the last complete survey (1967—8) it was calculated that 40% of all UK basic research was carried out in universities, 35% in government establishments, 20% in industry and 5% in other organisations.

6. Total R & D expenditure in the Netherlands is about one-sixth of that of the USA (and about one-quarter in per head of population terms). As has been described, nearly two-thirds of US R & D expenditure goes on 'atomic, space and defense research'; expenditure on such research in the Netherlands, however, as the article states, is 'insignificant compared with the Pentagon's' — in fact it represents only 5% of the Netherlands R & D budget. Thus in no way can Philips be dependent, as many aerospace and arms firms are in the USA and the UK, on government money to enable it to carry out R & D. However, Valery's comment that for Philips, 'Occasionally defense contracts help to remove the risk element' in research, raises an interesting general point.

We have already mentioned in Chapter 2 that, as far as this book is concerned, we do not consider atomic, space and defense research to be 'economically motivated'. Governments spend such large amounts of money on this type of R & D because they consider it necessary to defend the 'nation' or because such research is in some way prestigious. Whether they decide to spend such large amounts by their own choice or are persuaded to by those firms who will benefit most from the expenditure is a point we cannot investigate in detail (though see Proxmire, 1970). However it is clear that since it requires 'a great deal of entrepreneurial courage' for firms to invest large sums in doing adequate development work to enable profitable production of some new electronic device to be undertaken, the firm concerned will not be adverse to accepting (and even prompting the offer of) government money. It could be said then, that, whatever may be the reasons which persuade governments to make money available for defense R & D, it is possible for national security or prestige reasons to *coincide* with the economically determined requirements of the firm being contracted to do the R & D.

7. The ideas mentioned in this paragraph — 3D colour TV sets, two-way cable TV, TV newspapers, video cassette recorders and discs — are technologically exciting (at least we think so). Philips are keen to emphasise how advanced their thinking is. In summer 1974 they conducted an advertising campaign in various magazines. One of these ads contained a picture of two small, naked children and proclaimed:

AS ANY FOUR YEAR OLD WILL APPRECIATE, WE'RE MAKING SOME REMARKABLE TECHNOLOGICAL BREAK-THROUGHS.
Many of the things we're doing today will only be fully appreciated when today's children have grown up.
It's important to us that we give them a world of promise in which many of the pressing problems of today have been tackled.
This is not merely an ideal.
Every year, we spend over £200 000 000 in research and development.
To protect the environment, we've developed computer controlled monitoring devices that keep an electronic eye on the atmosphere.
To help save energy, we've made a 50% more efficient lamp.
To help fight cancer, we've built a new generation of X-ray machines and linear accelerators.
To help feed the world, we've produced new vitamins, antibiotics and vaccines for the mass treatment of livestock.
These are only a few of the things we're doing to make the future world a better one.
We've also provided teachers with a wide range of electronic teaching aids.

We've given computer manufacturers sophisticated miniaturised components.

We've produced new video recording and audio systems.

And, of course, hundreds of other products you use in your home every day.

PHILIPS

Simply years ahead.

In the notes to these two articles we have mentioned repeatedly the problem of long term interests of society versus the short term interests of individual firms as expressed in R & D activities. Does Philips' concern with the technologies that today's four year olds will be experiencing when they grow up indicate that the problem we posed is a false one?

We cannot hope to answer such a question in detail. Instead we give a number of further associated questions which can form the basis for discussion.

1. How does Philips, or any other company, *know* what we (or the four year olds) will want in 1984? Certainly the things Philips mention in their ad (protecting the environment, saving energy, fighting cancer, feeding the world) are highly commendable aims and no one can deny that they provide suitable areas in which research and development can produce results. But some results may be more fruitful than others. 'Technological breakthroughs' can be of many different kinds and so the actual innovations which Philips introduce may be the perfectly well-intentioned attempts to solve some of the problems of the world but are nevertheless innovations which *they* choose.

2. Do firms like Philips in fact really respond to people's needs (whatever they are) or do they create these needs first?

The American economist Galbraith (1974) maintains that the very size and cost of the techniques used by present day large companies forces them to persuade the consumer that what he or she wants to buy is what the firm's technology has been installed to produce. He sums up his analysis of contemporary industrial society thus:

> In virtually all economic analysis and instruction, the initiative is assumed to lie with the consumer. In response to wants that originate within himself, or which are given to him by his environment, he buys goods and services in the market. The opportunities that result for making more or less money are the message of the market to producing firms. They respond to this message of the market and thus, ultimately, to the instruction of the consumer. The flow of instruction is in one direction — from the individual to the market to the producer. All this is affirmed, not inappropriately, by terminology that

implies that all power lies with the consumer. This is called consumer sovereignty. There 'is always a presumption of consumer sovereignty in the market economy'. The uni-directional flow of instruction from consumer to market to producer may be denoted the *accepted sequence*.

We have seen that this sequence does not hold. And we have now isolated a formidable apparatus of method and motivation causing its reversal. The mature corporation has readily at hand the means for controlling the prices at which it sells as well as those at which it buys. Similarly, it has means for managing what the consumer buys at the prices which it controls. This control and management is required by its planning. The planning proceeds from use of technology and capital, the commitment of time that these require and the diminished effectiveness of the market for specialized technical products and skills (p. 216).

For proof of this he appeals to 'the evidence of the eye':

The eye sees a vast advertising and sales effort employing elaborate science and art to influence the customer. It sees huge sums expended for this effort, an estimated $19.6 billion for advertising in 1969. It senses great and subtle effort by the aerospace and like industries to persuade the armed services to want what they can supply. It sees a wholly unsubtle process by which the Pentagon instructs the Congress on what it wishes to have. Those who say that what is so seen cannot be proven are, in effect, saying that nothing can be proven. They are using a pseudo-scientific syllogism to avert attention from reality. (p. 15).

In other words it could be said that what you will want in 1984 are what Philips and GEC (and other large companies) say you will want.
3. How can R & D be organised so it is directed towards what people want? Defenders of the current modes of organisation (like those who defend the concept of consumer sovereignty, castigated by Galbraith) maintain that people *do* get what they want and that R & D is organised to come up with new ideas aimed at satisfying their market-conveyed wants. Others, pointing to those aspects of life which are not catered for by the market system (like the effects on the environ-ment or the safety of employees) suggest that the short term goals of large companies (to keep profitable) inevitably distort R & D organisation so that the longer term needs of society cannot be catered for.

Points for discussion or essays

1. Compare and contrast GEC's and Philips research and development policies.

2. In the light of the article on GEC and the letter from ASTMS what do you think would and should be the attitude of (i) GEC employees (ii) GEC's shareholders (iii) 'society at large' to GEC's R & D policy?

3. Is the patent system 'a good thing'?

4. Portable electronic calculators are, at the time of writing, enjoying a tremendous sales boom and technical developments have brought their price down to a point where it seems that a sophisticated machine will soon be comparable in price with a pound of beef. Discuss this phenomenon in terms of 'what the public wants'. How wide a range of alternatives is the public given?

Appendix One
Reading

The following works are referred to in the text, those of most general importance being asterisked.

Allen, T.J. (1970). Communication Networks in R & D Laboratories, *R and D Management*, 1, 1

Carter, C.F. and Williams, B.R. (1957). *Industry and Technical Progress*, Oxford; O.U.P.

Central Statistical Office (1973). *Research and Development Expenditure*, London; H.M.S.O.

Child, J. (1969). *The Business Enterprise in Modern Industrial Society*, London; Collier-Macmillan

Counter-Information Services (1972). *The GEC Anti-Report*, London; Counter-Information Services

Denison, E. and Poullier, J. (1968). *Why Growth Rates Differ*, London; Allen and Unwin

Elliott, D. and Elliott, R. (1976). *The Control of Technology*, Wykeham

*Freeman, C. (1974). *The Economics of Industrial Innovation*, London; Penguin

*Galbraith, J.K. (1974). *The New Industrial State*, 2nd Ed, London; Penguin

Jewkes, J., Sawers, D. and Stillerman, R. (1969). *The Sources of Invention*, p. 207, London; Macmillan

Jones, R. and Marriott, O. (1970). *Anatomy of a Merger*, London; Jonathan Cape

*Langrish, J., Gibbons, M., Evans, W.G. and Jevons, F.R. (1972). *Wealth from Knowledge: A Study of Innovation in Industry*, London; Macmillan

*Mansfield, E. (1968). *The Economics of Technological Change*, New York; Norton

Mansfield, E. (1968). *Industrial Research and Technological Innovation*, New York; Norton

Marquis, D.G. and Myers, S. (1970). *Successful Industrial Innovation*, National Science Foundation

Nabseth, L. and Ray, G.F. (1974). *The Diffusion of New Industrial Process*, Cambridge; C.U.P.

*Norris, K. and Vaizey, J. (1973). *The Economics of Research and Technology*, London; George Allen and Unwin

Proxmire, W. (1970). *Report from Wasteland*, New York; Praeger

Rosenberg, N. (ed) (1971). *The Economics of Technological Change*, London; Penguin

*Salter, W.E.G. (1960). *Productivity and Technical Change*, Cambridge, C.U.P.

Schon, D. (1967). *Technology and Change,* London; Pergamon Press

Sklair, L. (1973). *Organised Knowledge,* Paladin

*Science Policy Research Unit (1972). *Success and Failure in Industrial Innovation: Report on Project Sappho,* Centre for the Study of Industrial Innovation

Turner, G. (1971). *Business in Britain,* London; Penguin

*Williams, B.R. (1967). *Technology, Investment and Growth,* London; Chapman and Hall

The following short list is of books which are considered to be of interest and value.

Carter, D.F. and Williams, B.R. (1957). *Industry and Technical Progress,* Oxford; O.U.P; (1958) *Investment in Innovation,* Oxford; OUP; (1959). *Science in Industry,* Oxford; OUP

These three books are the result of the earliest, modern, studies on the relationship between science, technology, innovation and economic growth. The first book presents an analysis of what determines the speed of application of new scientific and technical knowledge in British Industry, the results of a study of 250 firms. The second deals with the problems of how decisions to spend money on capital equipment were made and the third presents 'proposals for action' for industry and government to help them formulate policies to increase economic growth by a better use of research and development.

Dickson, D. (1974). *Alternative Technology: Politics of Technical Change,* London; Fontana

Langrish, J. (1972). 'University Chemistry Research: Any Use to Industry?' *Chemistry in Britain,* **8,** 8

Mansfield, E. et al. (1972). *Research and Innovation in the Modern Corporation,* London; Macmillan

In this book are reported the findings of a number of studies on various aspects of the economics of technological change, focussing on the attempts of individual American firms to develop and utilise new technology. There are particularly interesting (though specialist) chapters on 'Innovation and Discovery in the Drug Industry' and 'The Diffusion of a Major Manufacturing Innovation' (viz. Numerical-controlled machine tools).

National Bureau of Economic Research (ed) (1962). *The Rate and Direction of Inventive Activity: Economic and Social Factors,* Princeton; PUP

A collection of conference papers (many quite technical) on the relationship between technological change and economic growth. Contains interesting articles on technological developments in the Aluminium, Petroleum refining and Chemical industries.

Appendix Two
Glossary of Economic Terms
Used in Text

Capital: In the sense we use it, capital means any material inputs to a production process which are not labor, i.e. the machines, tools and raw materials on and with which labor operates.

Economic Growth: Is conventionally measured by changes in a country's Gross National Product (see below) although other measures might be selected as more appropriate for particular purposes.

Factors of Production: Are inputs to a production process. They can be divided into two groups — *capital* (see above) and *labor* (see below). At a lower level of aggregation it is possible to talk of, for example, pig-feed as a factor of production in the production of pork or the labor of first hand melters as a factor of production in the manufacture of steel. See below for a definition of *substitution*.

GNP or Gross National Product: Is defined as the total value of *all* goods and services produced in the economy over some period of time. It is a very imperfect measure of national well-being, even of strictly economic well-being; for example, if a man marries his housekeeper then GNP will decline!

Labor: See *factors of production.* Labor is the work that is performed on or with other factors of production. It is contributed by workers for that purpose.

Net output: See *turnover.* Net output of a firm or industry is the turnover less the cost of purchases of material and fuel.

Profits: Are the sums of money which a firm has left from sales revenues after meeting all costs of capital and labor. Quoted figures may be before or after tax is paid. *Distributed profits* are passed on to the shareholders while *retained profits* are used for investment.

Research intensity or R & D intensity: Is the amount of money that a firm or indurty spends on research and development expressed as a fraction (usually as a percentage) of *net output* (see above).

Substitution: Of factors of production, one for the other, is possible in most production processes, e.g. if extra labor is employed it may be possible to maintain output with fewer machines — *labor* has therefore been substituted for *capital*. The production function (see Chapter 1) for a technique is based on the substitution of factors of production.

Turnover: Of a firm is the total value of all sales of goods and work done. The turnover of an industry is calculated by aggregating the turnovers of individual firms. Since the outputs of some firms will be consumed as inputs to other firms some double counting will take place. *Net output* (see above) is therefore a more useful index for measuring the value of goods produced by an industry.

6714